COMMENTARIES ON
THE
GOSPEL OF THOMAS

Excerpts from the Marsanne talks

KARL RENZ

COMMENTARIES ON
THE
GOSPEL OF THOMAS

Excerpts from the Marsanne talks

❧

KARL RENZ

COMPILED BY
ANASUYA

EDITED BY
ANJALI WALSH

ZEN
PUBLICATIONS
A Division of Maoli Media Private Limited

Commentaries On The Gospel Of Thomas
Excerpts from the Marsanne talks

First Edition: December 2015

PUBLISHED BY

ZEN PUBLICATIONS
A Division of Maoli Media Private Limited

60, Juhu Supreme Shopping Centre,
Gulmohar Cross Road No. 9, JVPD Scheme,
Juhu, Mumbai 400 049. India.

Tel: +91 90222 08074
eMail: info@zenpublications.com
Website: www.zenpublications.com

Book Design: Red Sky Designs, Mumbai
Cover Image: 'The Incredulity of Saint Thomas', 1603, by the renowned artist Caravaggio

ISBN   978-93-85902-00-0

Contents

❧

Other Books by Karl Renz

- Undecided: *Neti-Neti*

- A Little Bit Of Nothingness
  81 Observations On The Unnamable

- The Song of Irrelevance
  Meditation of what you are

- Heaven and Hell

- Am I - I Am

- May It Be As It Is
  The Embrace of Helplessness

- Worry and be Happy
  The Audacity of Hopelessness

- Echoes of Slience
  Avadhut Gita Revisited

- If You Wake Up, Don't Take It Personally
  Dialogues in the Presence of Arunachala

- The Myth of Enlightenment
  Seeing Through the Illusion of Separation

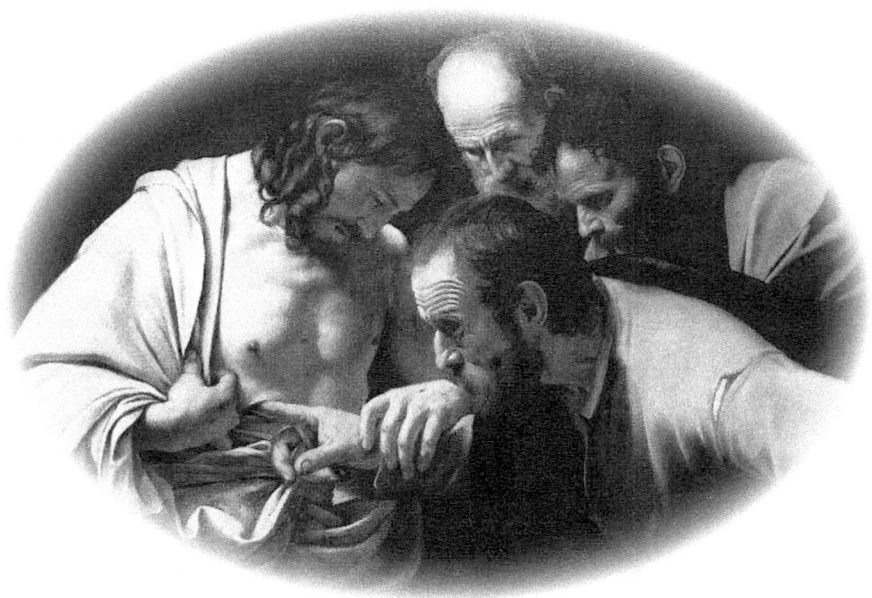

INTRODUCTION

❧

DISCOVERY OF THE GOSPEL OF THOMAS

A round 1945, in the area of Nag Hammadi in Upper Egypt, some peasants accidentally discovered some fifty-three parchments written in Sahidic Coptic buried in a large jar one meter high. Those leather-bound papyrus codices were mostly Gnostic texts, including the prestigious "Gospel of Thomas": this manuscript is dated 4th century A.D. but quite possibly is a Coptic translation from Greek, the traces of which have been found in very damaged papyri discovered in Oxyrhynchus, Hellenic city of Middle Egypt, dated 3rd century A.D.

The Gospel of Thomas is composed of 114 logia (plural of logion) or sayings from Jesus, which reveal that the Kingdom is already present in each of us contrary to the canonical Gospels which advocate an apocalyptic psychosis in an eschatological context. This is because Gnosis, free from all religions, doesn't know any spatiotemporal otherworldliness.

"Between the time when Jesus lived and the time when his words have definitely been fixed in the canonical Gospels, there have been multiple and deep reshuffles in the text", one can read in the introduction of "L'Évangile de Thomas" translated from

English and commentary by Émile Gillabert, Pierre Bourgeois and Yves Haas. The original English translation quoted in this book is by Thomas O. Lambdin and has been chosen due to its earnestness and authenticity. *"Meanwhile our humble Gnostics were meditating on the WORDS that since Thomas their scribes had faithfully been recopying on new papyri as soon as the old ones started to wear out. Until the day when, threatened by destruction as the result of their non-submission to the Judeo-Christian proselytes, they decided to preserve, if not their lives, at least their library, including of course the Thomas Gospel – which was the most important document – in its last and truthful copy. Thus, this treasure was entrusted to the Earth for some fifteen centuries…"*

No need to say that this discovery brought up a lot of polemics especially as at least half of the 114 logia are not to be found in the Gospels of the New Testament and those which do appear there are never exactly the same. Very different from the canonical Gospels, this remarkable text, which identifies Jesus as a Gnostic, is inviting us to a discovery of ourselves by ourselves through Life itself, which is our reality. Thus Christians and Gnostics are separated by an abyss. In the Christian tradition Gnostic texts have been banned and destroyed, and the texts found in this jar appeared on the list of a decree from bishop Athanasius of Alexandria ordering their destruction…

Today the discovery of the parchments from Nag Hammadi enables us to hear the voice of the Gnostics, victims of persecutions, whose writings strongly emphasized the primacy of individual direct experience.

DIDYMUS JUDAS THOMAS

It is said in the Prologue of the "Gospel of Thomas": *"These are the secret sayings, which the living Jesus spoke and which Didymus Judas Thomas wrote down."* In his commentaries, Émile Gillabert writes concerning Didymus Judas Thomas: *"The disciple habitually called Thomas is called here Didymus Judas Thomas, name not unknown from the Gospel of John. Didymus (Didumos in Greek) means "twin". This word probably refers to the quality and privilege of confidante and revealer of Jesus' message: As twin, Thomas is somehow Jesus' alter ego"*. Regarding Judas, Émile Gillabert spoke in length about this character to whom he has dedicated a book: "Judas, traître ou initié" (Judas, traitor or initiate).

THE METANOÏA ASSOCIATION

Émile Gillabert has been particularly fascinated by the Gospel of Thomas. He used to say that in India, Japan and China, there has been a plethora of non-dual texts while those were lacking in Western cultures. The discovery of the Gospel of Thomas has been providing the proof that Jesus uttered non-dual words attesting to the same awakening as the great sages of the East. Thus the source was also to be found in our Western tradition but had been concealed by centuries of theology. This is why Émile Gillabert has been rather particular on the correct French translation of this text in the light of the universal Gnosis, that is to say of the non-duality, so much so that he founded the Metanoia association whose purpose is to explore the Gospel of Thomas in depth as well as to make it known.

KARL RENZ

A few decades after Émile Gillabert' death, the Metanoia association had the fortunate inspiration to invite Karl Renz on four occasions, in 2003, 2005, 2008 and 2010. During those informal and spontaneous conversations, the participants had the opportunity to present to Karl a large number of logia in order to spark off his commentaries. This book tells the best part of those commentaries revealing Karl's responses to his questioners while expressing, over the course of the talks and in his unequivocal manner, the living Word which he so clearly embodies.

Whilst Karl's commentaries directly respond to each logion, they also answer participants' questions as they naturally come up and this free flow (which follows on from each logion as a spider web which is spun and then tightens itself) takes hold of the one who is exposing himself by blocking off all possible escape routes, thus creating an unconventional non-dual echo of the true Gnosis.

"We must – as Jesus suggests – divest ourselves of personal clothes. The necessity of this surrender is emphasized through all the 114 logia", Émile Gillabert stressed, agreeing with Karl: *"That is absolute nudity, And That is Jesus"*.

LOGION 57

Jesus said:
The kingdom of the father is like a man
who had good seed.
His enemy came by night
and sowed weeds among the good seed.
The man did not allow them to pull up the weeds;
he said to them, 'I am afraid that you will go intending
to pull up the weeds and pull up the wheat along with them.'
For on the day of the harvest
the weeds will be plainly visible,
and they will be pulled up and burned.

Since the original commentaries did not follow any precise order nor logical sequence, the logia appear in this book as they came up during the talks.

– Anasuya

These are the secret sayings
which the living Jesus spoke
and which Didymus Judas Thomas wrote down.

PROLOGUE OF THE GOSPEL OF THOMAS

Jesus is always the living word.
KARL RENZ

❧

1

I am That what is Jesus

❧

And he said:
Whoever finds the interpretation of these sayings
will not experience death.

Here it is about the inner Jesus and not the anecdotal Jesus of the appearances.

Actually we end up saying: "I am Jesus".

"I am that what is Jesus". It's different. Jesus said: "I am that what is the Father but I am not the Father". This always points to the essence of what is without naming it. So I will say: "I am That what is Jesus " and not "I am Jesus".

Doesn't it mean "I am That"?

When God descended from the skies and Moses asked him "Who are you?", he said: "I am what I am". So he specified he was the essence of the "I am". That what is consciousness but not this consciousness.

Which would imply that the individual stays...

No, no, it's the opposite. In fact it is eliminating it. It eliminates the definition. Again, Jesus is a name, a definition. Whereas you are empty. You are the emptiness where is the nature of Christ. In this tradition it is said that the nature of Christ is the essence. Same in Buddhism, the nature of Buddha is the essence, the Self. It's just another name for the Self.

It is important to specify what we mean by some words.

Yes and that's why I say: "I am That what is" and not: "I am Jesus" or "I am God", I don't name it. There is a book of Nisargadatta, which has the title: "I am That", which leaves That totally open. It eliminates the world. It's only points to what is prior to the phenomenal world, and always refers to the noumenon. To what cannot be named nor framed.

There is no different Selves. Even if That seems to be covered, That actually cannot be covered. There is no cover, no veil. Even if That appears to be forgotten for some times, covered by a religion, a tradition, That is always underlying, That is always present and That will show up again. In all traditions there are mystics and metaphysicians who stand at the top of the pyramid and from there look at the religions. Ways are infinite but they all lead to what you are. Because they all are made by the Self, for the Self. So you cannot miss your Self. What is the best way? I cannot tell. When you are at the top, there never has been any way. But it's not a competition. Every step always moves towards what you are. There is no way better than another. Self knows the best and there is nothing but the Self.

When religions go through periods of great deviations to the point of apparently losing all meaning, is that still a way?

Sometimes a detour is a direct way. Sometimes what seems to be a direct way is an infinite way. Who decides? Who sets the standards? What seems so long is nothing for what you are. It is out of time and what is in time will never become what is prior to time.

Jesus' message is an inner message, he tells us that the Self is inside of us in the secret cave, that is the truth. Yet two thousand years ago we took hold of Jesus to make a religion out of him. Paul de Tarse, called Saint-Paul, invented an absurd religion totally at the opposite of his master's message because he promised the salvation of the individual in another world. It's Disney world!

Yes, perfect.

And for two thousand years millions of human beings have been in a dead end!

But if you speak this way it's because you still see some one who can enter in a dead end. But for what you are, it makes no difference, "to reach what you are" has no meaning. So everything that this power has done was exactly what consciousness or God wanted this power to do. One cannot be mislead. And as long as you are somebody who can be misled...

Do you mean that everything that comes out of the Self has no existence?

It's a reflection. But it's not the Self. And in this reflection they are infinite reflections, ways which lead and ways which mislead. So any idea of being misled needs some one who can be misled. And this first thought "I" is already a falsity in itself. Whether it says "this leads me" or " this misleads me", both are false. As soon as this thought "I" rises the concept is there, and everything that comes out of it misleads. There will never be somebody who can be led to the right path. The very idea of right path creates the wrong path.

So there is no good nor evil. Everything is ok. Then Saint Paul has a role in the scheme of the Self.

In Tibetan Buddhism those who keep the religion or the teachings alive are called the Dharma keepers. For this we need techniques, paths and everything that can be done so that this world can exist. It simply is a functioning, which preserves this world. There is nothing true nor false in this, that's not the question. For whom should it be true or false?

Whatever you name, you give it life. When you say "illusion", this illusion is there. And whatever you will do with it will make it real. The simple fact of uttering "illusion" makes it real. It needs somebody to say that something is an illusion but this somebody is already an illusion. The one who defines himself is a definition. Then whatever comes from this first definition, whatever somebody says makes no difference for what you are. To name something cannot make you what you are. This understanding that the world is an illusion comes and goes, but not what you are and you don't depend on this understanding or realisation that all this is a dream. Whatever name you give to it, it's just another concept.

I am in full agreement with what you just said. It's a total illusion to imagine that it may be a path. So everything which is separate, starting with the individual, is illusory, it has no existence. Yet I appear to be in this improved pithecanthropus' body.

Yes, but Jesus said: As man I am an absolute man. As Spirit I am an absolute Spirit. And as source I am the absolute source. Because I am the Absolute in whatever circumstances. It makes no differences.

LOGION 77

Jesus said:
It is I who am the all.
From me did the all come forth,
and unto me did the all extend.

So be this Absolute here and now and there is no body, no world, nothing but the Self. Because there is no one in this body and no one out of this body. There is only the Self. Whatever form it takes, it doesn't change anything. So be the absolute Self, that's all.

Nothing makes a difference for what you are. All differences are different forms of what you are but they don't make you different in any way. You are the Absolute, which takes different forms but never changes. So there is nobody in this body and in this very moment you are this body as consciousness in a form and there is no difference because only consciousness is, here and now.

So in this body I am always perfection.

There is no one who is perfect. There is only perfection.

This goes back to what you were saying: There is no Jesus but "what is Jesus". The divergence between those two expressions is only apparent because when we say "I am Jesus" it is not connected to Jesus as a person.

No, no, actually it's a mistake, a total mistake. Because if you say that you are free, you again define yourself and stay as "me", but you are not liberated. You are absolute in the non-knowledge of what you are or what you are not. This is what you are, totally in the mystery of what you are or what you are not. Totally undecided about what you are or what you are not.

This neither excludes nor includes anything. It is to be free of any definition, even of the idea of freedom. Because there is nobody who needs freedom, nobody who ever had the slightest need. "Be what you are" simply means "Be this Absolute", which you can neither lose nor gain. And this only is peace, when nobody is left.

❧

2

The moment you think you are born, you are dead

❦

Jesus said:
Whoever has come to understand the world
has found (only) a corpse,
and whoever has found a corpse
is superior to the world.

What is the use of this manifestation? For which purpose is this perfection putting itself in such poverty?

But which Self is in a state of poverty? An idea is an idea, an idea of poverty or whatever idea makes no difference. The manifestation has no utility and that is its beauty because it has no meaning. It is freedom itself, free from meaning, free from a cause. It is simply the realization of what is real but not because of a need, nor a meaning, nor a will. It is an absence of desire, which simply realizes itself through the realization but not for any reason. That is its beauty, its pure beauty.

You can say that it is a dance. The dance of the Self. Like Shiva dancing with himself in this *shakti*, this realization. And to be what is Shiva, to dance with what you are is to be Life itself dancing with itself. Thus there is no poverty, there is nothing. All this comes from the idea of "me" who wants to avoid suffering and only have pleasure.

I think that children express this very well.

Yes, they construct and then destroy. Without any worry. They don't accumulate in the name of a so-called poverty. But the moment the idea of possession rises you become a caretaker, this little caretaker who is so afraid of losing because he thinks he is owning something. The great caretaker of "my body", my corpse. And if you try to do something with it, you give life to what is already dead.

But what we are used to consider as dead are mental productions - namely ideas - and not the objects themselves. Because after all do objects exist apart from the idea we have of them?

This is still the idea of being born. And the moment you think you are born, you are dead. As long as you think you are alive you are dead, because then that what is life is but an idea to be alive. There is no objective life, this objective life is the life of the dead. So you go to the place of the dead - what the world is - simply because of this idea of being born. You become mortal. The idea of birth brings the idea of death. Be what is unborn, that can never die. Nothing else.

If I am, I am the infinite.

You are more than the infinite. The infinite is still too little for what you are. Whatever you say that you are is never big enough. And whatever you say that you are not is never small enough. Whatever we say are always concepts. Even if I say: "The absence of all concepts of what I am or what I am not", again it is simply a pointer. Eventually you stay quiet. There is no more definition. Even the most intelligent definition doesn't mean anything because definitions come and go. But you play with them. It is neither good nor bad. It is simply a game.

To go back to where you come from is to go back to what is prior. It is like Ramana Maharshi's question "Who am I?", to dive into this mystery. You come from That which is the Self, the Absolute, whatever name you give to it. Then you wake up as "I", the awareness, then as "I am", space, time, consciousness, then as "I am so and so", the man. And to return to where you come from, there is the question "Who am I?". This, you do every night: when you go to sleep, the person drops, then the "I am", and the awareness stays. Then even the awareness... In deep deep sleep there is no experience. Then in the morning the "I" rises first, in a split second, then the "I am", then, oh..., the memory-body starts to work. And in the evening you return. So in deep deep sleep everyone knows who he is by not knowing it. So be here and now what is in deep deep sleep.

3
Be immobile, and you are the fastest

٭

LOGION 50

... If they ask you:
What is the sign of your father in you?
say to them:
It is movement and repose.

You are that what is totally immobile in itself. All this dreamlike movement happens around you. So when you travel, you are not going anywhere. You always are that what is totally immobile and places are coming to you.

It is said in the Mundaka Upanishad: He who doesn't move goes faster than he who runs.

Be immobile, and you are the fastest. It is like absolute speed. Take this Absolute as an absolute particle, an absolute awakening of speed, and absolute speed is immobility. The moment when an absolute movement starts, it is already there where it started. So it never moves. By creating this whole dream universe it starts to wake up, and this wakening is an absolute wakening. But it doesn't move because even in this absolute speed it is always immobile. So you are this Absolute, which never moves in this realization. Totally immobile.

What is absolute, the Father, realizes itself in movement and non-movement. It is like a cross. The movement is the horizontal part and the non-movement is the vertical Spirit. Such is the symbol. Then there is the intersection of the cross, the centre, which is the Heart of awareness. This is the whole realization of Reality as awareness - the vertical Spirit - and time.

The movement is the waves, the rest is the ocean, and all of this is still the ocean.

The ocean is the unity and the waves are the duality. It is a symbol of consciousness, which is movement and non-movement, but it is already the realization of Reality. To call Reality "ocean" is not quite exact. And what to say about the non-ocean? It is like for Being and non-being. Being is the cross and non-being is the absence. There is presence and then there is absence.

But that what is the absence is also that what is the presence. So in the presence there is an ocean of consciousness: there is the wave which is relative, then the non-movement which is the no-time of the ocean, the Spirit, and then the awareness. And in the non-being you are not less the ocean than the non-ocean but in this so-called presence, all is ocean. All of this is consciousness. But as you are in the presence as well as in the absence, ocean or non-ocean, for what you are what is there to do? That's why it is said that God knows neither the ocean nor the non-ocean.

Is the non-being free or not?

No. There is non-being only because the Absolute is. There is absence only because there is presence, but that what is the Absolute knows neither presence nor absence. It is presence and it is absence and it is neither one nor the other.

At one point does the non-being become the Being?

It always is That. Being and non-being are two sides of the same coin. Nothing appears in appearing and nothing disappears in disappearing.

You have been talking about awareness. Is it the same as the Absolute?

No, it is already an expression of the Absolute. You can say that it is the beginning and the end of the Absolute manifesting itself. You can say that it is the purest experience but the purest experience is not the experience of that what is the Absolute. Simply drop the idea of Absolute, and be.

Can we say that the Absolute is what is the simplest?

You can say: The Absolute is that what is the Nature that knows no nature. It is Nature, but since That knows no nature, That doesn't know what is natural and what is not natural. Only when there is a knower is there a definition of what is natural or not. And it is already too late. When the knower defines there are infinite ways to try to be final.

Awareness is already an imagination. It is the first and the last experience. But the absolute Experiencer, which is the eternal origin, is not an imagination. Awareness is already an experience, but Reality is already there before knowing itself as awareness. Reality is. And the realization starts with the awareness: to be awake.

Nobody realizes the Absolute.

There is nobody in the Absolute. There is only the Absolute. Since nobody owns the Absolute, nobody can be the Absolute. That will always be a paradox, for sure, and you are this paradox. Only a paradox doesn't need to explain itself because for that what is *para*, prior to all ideas, the paradox is what is in the presence as in the absence. For That there is no paradox. But for the intellect it is an insoluble koan. How could that 'what is not' be that 'what is'? You cannot understand this, you can only be it. That never makes a problem and That needs neither explanation nor to solve a koan.

Nisargadatta Maharaj said: "You are pure unknowing".

What metaphysics indicates is a mystery, which will never be unravelled because there is no second that you can grasp, there is not even one. That can never be a relative knowledge, it never is an object of knowledge. Whatever you can know is an object in time but That is not in time.

So those words are more destructive than constructive.

You build by destroying. You are what is left. It is called the abstract, the substratum. You are the substratum from which nothing can be subtracted any more. Even when the idea of second disappears, you are.

❧

4
What wakes up is still asleep

❧

Jesus said:
If those who lead you say to you:
See, the kingdom is in the sky,
then the birds of the sky will precede you.
If they say to you: It is in the sea,
then the fish will precede you.
Rather, the kingdom is inside of you,
and it is outside of you.
When you come to know yourselves,
then you will become known,
and you will realize that it is you
who are the sons of the living father.
But if you will not know yourselves,
you dwell in poverty
and it is you who are that poverty.

To think that there is an inside and an outside is only an idea. First you look outside hoping to find happiness in objects, like a new car, or in the family, etc. You are looking outside for harmony and you cannot find it. Because it will always be an imperfect harmony, underlying, depending. Inside it is the same. You go into the infinite inner dimension but there, no harmony either. There is only emptiness. It is always a non-finding, and not a finding inside.

I only want to point out that there is no finding either inside or outside. So you stay undecided because it is neither inside nor outside. Jesus said: I am that what is inside and I am that what is outside but I myself have no inside nor outside. It is always the *essence* of the inside and of the outside. There is no Jesus having an inside or an outside.

When awakening happens to a person can we say that consciousness becomes aware of itself?

There never has been a person on Earth and never will be. There never was a Buddha who walked on Earth neither a Jesus, who always emphasized that his Kingdom was not of this world. There never will be anybody. A concept cannot realize what is not a concept. And the Self doesn't need to be realized because the Self is always realized and has no need that a concept realizes what is the Self. So there never has been a realized person on Earth. Because the Self is all there is. There never has been a person, never ever.

Awakening doesn't happen, and what wakes up is still asleep. What has the idea to be awake is still sleeping. And that what is the Self knows no sleep nor awakening. Awareness has no idea of awakening. So there is no awakening, because this is the awareness which is always present. So spoke Master Eckhart: What you are doesn't know any coming or going. And what needs the coming and going of an awakening, comes and goes. So if a phantom wakes up to what is still a phantom, it makes no difference. It is a dreamer waking up in a dream, a dream in another dream. Because the one you call the dreamer, the experiencer, still belongs to the dream.

That what is the Self has never been concerned or unconcerned. This is called the eye of God, the inner eye, the absolute Experiencer, which is the Self. It never sleeps nor wakes. It is this space-like consciousness and whatever happens there is nothing but dream experiences. So this way whatever you can know or realize has no value. It doesn't make you what you are. Because what you are doesn't belong to what rises or to what wakes up to something. You can call this a total resignation of the Self, which will never know itself.

By wishing to know itself, the Self steps out of paradise. This is why Jesus said that he will not make this world a paradise and there will be wars and no satisfaction will be found.

LOGION 16

Jesus said:
Men think, perhaps,
that it is peace which I have come to cast upon the world.
They do not know
that it is dissension which I have come to cast upon the earth:
fire, sword, and war.

There can be no satisfaction in objects. And totally resigning from the idea that one will ever be able to find satisfaction in this objective world is what is called "the inner return": to turn towards that what is the source, towards perfection itself.

You look outside endlessly and you cannot find yourself. Then you look inside *ad infinitum* and you still cannot find yourself. So you rest in the non-finding. And this is total resignation, you don't search anymore for what you are. And in this rest, in this total immobility, there is perfection. Everything you were seeking is there, without any seeking. The seeker was already what he was seeking.

Can we say that awakening is always present and that the individual can only be aware of it when he disappears, so that he cannot be aware of it anymore?

The person cannot drop itself, never. It is the person who is dropped. It drops, that's all, like when you go to sleep. This awakening may be like falling asleep. This knowledge is totally addressed to what is unknown. To become totally what is unknown is to become that what is knowledge but without knowing it ever. Then you become the Essence of knowledge, which knows no knowledge. You become that what is the Self without knowing the Self. Hence the absence of self or absence of desire is called *sat-chit-ananda*, absolute happiness in the absolute absence of one who can be happy or unhappy and doesn't even know happiness. Nobody is happy in happiness. In the absence of you there is happiness. So see that this phantom "me" is simply a phantom unable to be happy.

5
No matter what you say,
I will say the opposite

ॐ

LOGION 71

Jesus said:
I shall destroy this house,
and no one will be able to build it.

*K*arl gives us a sense of perpetual movement and as soon as we
stop for thinking, for pondering, for rejoicing, for worrying,
we are mistaken.

Whatever you say, I will take an opposite point of view and
then I will destroy both of them. Here nothing can stay. No matter
what you say, I will say the opposite.

What strikes me is the movement. We often tend to stop for
an idea, a concept and we should never stop.

There is no need to stop anything. Because nothing moves.
Nothing ever happened. So what is there to stop? You are space itself
and in this space dream objects are passing by as consciousness.

Karl destroys all concepts as they appear as well as what he himself says, maybe so that we become aware that we are prior to concepts. It is this Knowledge that no word can define and about which nothing can be said.

I would say that no word can disturb this quietness. There is no need even to stay quiet because you cannot become more quiet than you already are and you cannot be disturbed by any mental noise whatsoever. Never mind the noise because you don't depend on tranquillity or anything else.

Can we say that when we are in the non-understanding we are in the Reality?

When you are that which is Reality the question of reality doesn't arise anymore. And as long as this question arises it is not Reality. But when there is Reality there is nothing but Reality: then it is an absence of questions, which means an absence of a questioner.

Can we still talk about realization, is there anyone who is realized?

No. This "one" who can be realized already belongs to the realization. But we can talk about the realization: it is now, and now, and now… Yet Reality is nowhere to be found.

Whatever you say is not That. Whatever you say belongs to the realization of Life but is not real. It is not different from Reality but it is not real. We can talk about life but Life doesn't know any life because what we call life is already the realization of Life. Whatever we experience, whatever we say belongs to the realization but not Reality.

Does Life come from nowhere, from nothingness, or is it always present?

Life never comes or goes. It is silence. Never born, it never dies. Without coming and going, it is without origin. You can say that it IS the origin but it has no origin. So it is the origin of whatever you can imagine but That, you cannot imagine. So you cannot make an image of it. Then again for the image to be there the origin must be there. For realization to be, Reality must be there. But we cannot find it, name it or frame it. So That is your nature and you cannot not be it, but you will never know it in a relative way. And whatever we can say is relative and part of the realization, of this dream. Whatever is your dream, you cannot find yourself in it because you never lost yourself in it. The idea that you can find yourself or that you already found yourself is called hell because it makes you an object in time, and makes you dependent.

So those beings who claim to be realized, who speak as realized beings, it is a dream!

One who claims that he is realized belongs to the dream. He belongs to hell because hell means differences. When there is one who is realized there is another one who is not realized and this is hell. In the Upanishads it is very clearly stated: One who claims he is a jnani is not a jnani. And one who claims he is a master needs to meet his master. This way, who can claim he is realized? Only in a dream are there realized beings. Therefore they are realized phantoms. And who cares about realized phantoms? Phantoms, who else!

Oh my God, a realized phantom! But who cares if one claims he is realized and the other not? Reality doesn't care. What difference does it make if one says he is realized and the other says he is not. Both statements are false! Whether they say they are realized or not both are what they are. No difference. Because you are That no matter what. You can claim whatever you like, who cares?

The only reason for claiming is the desire to be a teacher and dominate others. It is based upon hierarchy: "I know better than you, I am realized and you are not. My heart is open and yours is closed". All this is based upon differences of levels, it is a competition to know who is the highest.

If a disciple comes to see a master, obviously it is to ask for his advice. It is the master who participates in the game of the disciple.

Both are played by consciousness. Consciousness plays the master and the disciple, that's all. Nobody has consciousness, nobody plays, everybody is played. It is only a game. You can call that joy, a dance of energy, Life in action, whatever you like. And nothing happens. No problem.

Does the word "freedom" mean anything to you?

Absolutely but not relatively. Freedom is the nature of the Absolute and the Absolute never needs to be free. But freedom can never be reached. You cannot "attain" freedom and nobody will ever be free. Reality is freedom because there is no second: there is only Reality, so it cannot depend on anything else. In this world everything is dependence, even the idea of freedom makes you dependent. Simply drop the idea of freedom, and be!

I was wondering if there is a state that is free and if it is the state of being realized.

Yes, there is state of liberation: your nature. It is your natural state. Reality cannot be related to anything and nobody has ever been free in a different way... everyone's nature is freedom.

But can we say that Reality is free to realize itself or not?

No, Reality is not free in that sense. It must realize itself, it cannot not realize itself. Absolute Reality, which is the Absolute dreamer, cannot not dream. Although it is freedom, it has to realize itself. It is a paradox.

Freedom means there is no second. Such is freedom: free from a second reality but Reality is not free from the realization because the realization is the Reality by its nature. So there is no two. Since Reality is the realization it cannot avoid itself. So this is Life and Life cannot avoid Life. Hence it is freedom in action, the dance of freedom. Since the Self is imprisoned by the Self there is no prisoner. And nobody to care.

Since there is no two there is no dependence, no control. Since it is without a second by its nature, That cannot even control itself, because for control, you need two. So That is Almighty but has no power. That is energy but That cannot do anything, nor decide anything, nor want anything. That is omnipotent but totally unable to control anything. And this helplessness, which is a total absence of control, is freedom.

Nisargadatta said that Existence is like a film, which is predetermined down to the smallest detail: "Even what I am saying is predetermined since ever". Does freedom means no choice?

Freedom from choice. In fact free from the chooser! It is a block of Reality and realization, which is never never. So the next moment doesn't come and the last moment is not gone. Therefore it is like a film, frame by frame, infinite, like the symbol of the infinite.

Do concepts nevertheless have a reality as illusion?

Everything is there. The nature of any concept is Reality. The origin of concepts is the Absolute, so their nature is the Absolute but concepts are not the Absolute. The nature of this microphone is energy but the microphone is not energy.

Freedom is freedom from choice. Freedom cannot want what it wants. Some philosophers, like the Austrian Ludwig Wittgenstein, have stated that even God cannot want what he wants, so what to say? No, That is as it is, no more no less, and you will never know what it is.

One who has to realize himself has already a designed path from birth. Nothing has to be changed.

Nobody will ever be realized. Reality is ever realized, and this fleeting "me" who belongs to the realization will never be able to realize Reality. There never was an enlightened being nor an unenlightened being. Life has always been Life. Reality is always Reality. No need to realize That because That realizes itself in everything that is! And what belongs to the realization can never become the origin of it. Otherwise we could as well say "can a stone realize Life"? No! You are Life and you realize yourself, but you can never realize That, which realizes Itself. You are always realized, no more no less. Therefore That will never appear and That has never disappeared. There is no such thing as more or less realization. The next sip of coffee is the realization of what you are. There will never be big fireworks nor final understanding nor deep silence. All this belongs to the realization and cannot make you more real than you already are. There is no such thing as more or less real.

There is no such thing as "the real and the illusion", there is only Reality.

Illusion is only that you can find Reality in the realization, that you can realize yourself. This is illusion, because if you could realize yourself, you would be different from what you are. You cannot realize what you are, thanks God, even if you have to keep realizing yourself in the realization. Whatever you realize is your realization but it's not what you are. So you must be That what is the unknown and even if whatever you may know is not different from it, it is not what you are. The un-pronounced which is pronounced is never what is pronounced but always what pronounces it, and it can never pronounce the very thing which pronounces. And while I am pronouncing that, even that is...

These are just pointers. There never has been a realized person: what a joy! And you will not be the first one! If there never was a realized person your idea that you are not realized disappears as well. As long as there is a possibility to realize yourself you must constantly justify yourself: "Am I really ready? Did I do enough? Is my understanding deep enough? Is my devotion high enough? Am I really honest?" What a constant pressure! But if you see: "Ah... I will never be enlightened!", phew, what a relief!

I am speaking about the joy of not being able to know yourself. For me, when I speak about joy it indicates that I don't need to be joyful. I don't need to relax, phew, what a relaxation! I don't need to open myself, closed or open, no difference! I don't need to be happy! Enjoy the happiness of not having to be happy. Be independent from happiness!

6
You cannot be more naked than you already are

✤

LOGION 4

Jesus said:
The man old in days will not hesitate
to ask a small child seven days old
about the place of life,
and he will live.
For many who are first will become last,
and they will become one and the same.

You are this small child. You try to grow up but never succeed. So be That which never grows because you are not something which can grow. Whatever can grow is not what you are.

This is pointing to this Knowledge that you never lost because it is not an object that you can lose. You don't need to care about it or to make effort to attain it. This non-knowing is your nature, which cannot be gained or lost. This is freedom. But for whatever understanding, whatever possession, whatever realization that you can gain, so much effort! Then you must preserve and polish those pearls of understanding. I am too lazy for that, thanks God. If you need this Knowledge be the most lazy, for it never does anything.

This makes me think of the small child who doesn't know anything.

Don't try to make anything out of it such as looking like a child or whatever. When Jesus says: "Become like a small child", it means: simply be what you are before the age of three because then there is no possession, there is no such thing as "my body" or "my life". Go to this absence of owner because freedom is where nothing is "yours" nor "not yours". It is indicating this nature which is yours and doesn't need to understand to be what it is. Existence itself is Knowledge and no understanding can add anything to it.

But isn't it said in this logion 4: "The man old in days will not hesitate to ask a small child seven days old about the place of life, and he will live"?

This means that you cannot give enlightenment. Your nature cannot be given, that's all. That what is Shiva, your nature, always wants to play, so it will play. When Grace happens it is to behead you whether you enjoy the game or not and not because you are ready or because you don't want to play any more. It comes by surprise and not by your wishes. And if somebody wants to give it to you, ha-ha, be careful! Nobody can give Grace. On the contrary, when Grace comes it's more like a rape. It takes you like nothing. For Grace shows no mercy and your head will be cut off whether you like it or not. When harvest time has come the corn has nothing to say. Nobody will ask you: Are you ready, would you enjoy it?

No, you are That what is Grace and Grace cannot decide on the moment when it will show its mercilessness and tear everything that can be torn. The veil will be torn when it will be torn because by nature there is no necessity that anything goes.

With the example of the small child Jesus wants to take away everything that is not my timeless Reality and makes me understand that I am not a person but the Absolute.

Naked, Existence is naked in spite of the clothes! Anyhow the last shirt has no pockets. Every experience is like a shirt. When this hard disk which is the body will drop, erasing happens as if nothing ever happened. Hence be now what you are. Nakedness has put a coat on but under the coat you are naked. And the first coat is awareness. Of course those are just images.

Since childhood everyone has been experiencing countless situations and extreme circumstances but in spite of all this, Perception never changed. The perceiver changes with his story, through every experience, but the Perception in which the perceiver appeared has never been changed by all the changes he went through. This is called "the eye of God", which is the seeing *per se*, never changed, never increased nor diminished by what it sees. This is the nakedness of the child mentioned in the Gospel.

So there is still a hope for me...

Hope dies last! The idea of "me" comes from the hope to know oneself and when this hope disappears the "me" vanishes. Without hope, no "me". Jesus calls this "the dark night of the soul", when all hope disappears, all meaning, all purpose, when you become aware that the world cannot make you happy. Then a holocaust, which is the awareness of this, eradicates this idea of separation. And only this awareness is the Grace, which cannot be reached by anyone.

Grace tears you away in spite of yourself. You cannot do anything for or against it. It doesn't know you. It is absolutely merciless, ready to devour. The infinite is always present but only when this armour, this idea of separation, weakens, does Grace seize you. Most people experience the dark night of the soul as a deep depression, a total void of all sense, all ideas. In this emptiness of meaning and purpose the person is eradicated. This is Grace.

Unfortunately when this happens we tend to take Prozac or antidepressants.

So it is not supposed to happen. Because this survival system, the "me", will do anything to avoid it. The "me" always tries to avoid emptiness. He is constantly filling what is empty by any idea. That is his survival system. This concept "me" has to create problems so that this problem "me" can remain, and emptiness is his biggest problem. The absence of problems is the biggest problem for this problem "me". And he is very creative, as creative as the Self! He has all the power of the Self to maintain this separation that he takes for real. He has the all-mighty power of consciousness to remain in this idea of separation.

Unless the divine accident happens... Then even if you have your driving licence it will not prevent you from crashing into a tree. Bang! You must be totally drunk with yourself not to know anymore which direction you take. Out of control, totally drunk with what you are, you don't know anymore what you are doing!

But for this one who doesn't know what he is doing, for the "poor in spirit" who doesn't know what he is and what he is not, it is paradise. Again it is the nakedness from ideas, which cannot be made. You cannot undress yourself to be naked because you cannot be more naked than you already are. Every idea which makes you believe that you can do something to become That is a concept that you put on.

❧

7

You don't see the Living because it doesn't move

๛

The disciples said to Jesus:
We know that you will depart from us.
Who is to be our leader?"
Jesus said to them:
Wherever you are,
you are to go to James the righteous,
for whose sake heaven and earth came into being.

If such is their interest disciples have to turn towards those concerned by the world.

What strikes me in this logion is that Jesus accepts any attitude from the disciples.

Jesus accepts everything because he is the source of all. He does it effortlessly.

James who happened to be Jesus' brother is said to have been the first leader of the Church of Jerusalem. Regarding religions you say that in the end, whether there is attachment to a religion or not, it is almost the same.

I would not say that it is the same but it is always adapted to the situation, to the culture. It is always a matter of adaptation.

Being the One I don't have to worry about what others do, if I may say so. On the contrary I totally don't care if the Catholic, Protestant or Islamic religions have different visions or dogmas.

It shows the direction. One must stay concentrated on himself because it is not through others that one finds himself. Whether there is another or not, we are always here. On the other hand Jesus says not to care about the dead. "Let the dead bury their own dead 1". It goes in the same direction.

(1) Luke 9:60.

And in logion 52, when the 24 prophets are being mentioned to him, Jesus answers:

> *You have omitted the one living in your presence
> and have spoken (only) of the dead.*

You don't see the Living because it doesn't move.

Jesus' words are as daring as yours, when you say: Everything is here. No need to look elsewhere.

Everything is complete. No need to change anything.

For me, at this very moment, the Living is here.

As always. "For where two or three gather in my name, there am I with them 1". It is the concentration of the movement towards the unmoving and this is what the Gnosis is: A snake looks at his own tail and thinks, because it doesn't move, that it is another snake. But in reality only his own tail is moving.

(1) Matthew 18:20.

Understanding that what is moving is not different from what is unmoving is the knowledge of the Self. He who is silent recognizes himself in the movement. Therefore nothing comes and goes. No difference. This is the Gnostic symbol of the snake which bites his own tail, there is nothing but the Self in the movement as in the non-movement. There is no contradiction.

Didn't you say that nothing moves, that everything is immobile? This would actually prove that there is no time nor space.

Paradox. Paradox.

So there is neither movement not rest. If nothing moves, everything is immobile.

There is no movement, no silence, no rest. We must say that we are that what is movement and are that what is silence and in that very instant the paradox vanishes, there is no more contradiction. The contradiction is there only when we define one or the other. When you are silence, you are silence and when you are movement, you are movement. But your Self never moves nor is silent.

LOGION 50

If they ask you:
What is the sign of your father in you?
Say to them:
It is movement and repose.

It is a whole: The movement as well as the silence, that what became light by itself. It is the Absolute. And at the end of the logion it is said that "it is movement and repose": the paradox is there. This is why the Hindu religion speaks about the paradox of Parabrahman: the absolute Being which is and which is not. It is always *para*, beyond. Therefore we also say *para-dise*, that what is prior.

The movement and the rest in Brahma are a paradox. But the movement and the rest prior to Brahma, Parabrahman, are no more a paradox because then all is resolved.

There is no solution or non-solution because it doesn't interest anyone. In the absence of a concept of understanding there is no necessity to understand. It is simply a paradox, a koan. It is not solved, it is simply no more there. A solution would already be another state but there is no solution. Dissolution is total annihilation.

I find that this logion 50 is an immense proof of love on behalf of Jesus: he is in unicity and is coming down to us with words, knowing they are only words.

Compassion is his nature, he doesn't need to talk to some one because there is no one to talk to.

But we are hearing him.

Jesus is talking to himself and listening to himself. He is hearing himself. There is no such thing as "speaking to some one" since there is no one to whom to talk.

When everything is lost there is nothing to lose any more.

Yes, we still can lose "what is already lost".

LOGION 41

*... and whoever has nothing
will be deprived of even the little he has.*

And we still can lose "one who has already lost everything". From this one, I take even what he doesn't have. I take away from him the ownership of "owning nothing". Because not having anything is still owning. Even from this one who doesn't know, it will be taken. First there is the knower, then the non-knower, until nothing remains, specially "one" for whom nothing remains.

8
The knowledge of absolute unknowing

❧

LOGION 67

Jesus said:
If one who knows the all
still feels a personal deficiency,
he is completely deficient.

If you know the world and all its secrets but you don't know yourself, you don't know anything. Even if you have understood everything, even if you have known everything that can be known, still you don't know yourself, on the grounds that whatever you can know is not what you are! When you know That what you are, you know that what is All.

In other words, even if all that can be known were known to you, you still wouldn't know anything because none of this has an effect on what you are. But the moment you know Yourself, in the non-knowing of what you are or of what you are not, you know All! This is the paradox of Knowledge: you know yourself in the Absolute not-knowing because you are That what is unknowable, you are the ungraspable, the incomprehensible, without a second. And any idea or possibility of knowing creates duality.

To be only That what doesn't know any second, to be the Absolute which has no idea of a second, to be That what is Absolute knowledge without knowing anything, because knowledge is always duality: This is the essence of Jesus' words.

Yet it is said in logion 3:

> *But if you will not know yourselves,*
> *you dwell in poverty*
> *and it is you who are that poverty.*

Yes, this is the paradox: the Absolute knowledge to be at this very moment That what is absolutely unknowable because there is no second. The understanding of non-duality is the knowledge of absolute non-knowing.

It is when we don't have this knowledge of non-knowing that we are in poverty.

It is always a matter of interpretation. In the literal sense we could give different interpretations. At one point Jesus says: "Blessed are the poor in spirit[1]". He means that if you meet someone who 'knows', you meet one who is ignorant. The absence of the idea of self is Knowledge. The absence of knowledge or non-knowledge is not the presence of somebody who knows or doesn't know: Knowledge is the absence of somebody who knows, namely the absence of an ignorant one. This implies all, nothing is excluded, because there, all questions about knowledge and non-knowledge dissolve.

(1) Matthew 5:3.

In other words we may listen to what you just said as well as not listen to it and not take it into account.

If you really don't worry about anything any more because the worrier is gone, then life is rich. But as long as there is somebody who worries about knowing, life is poor. It is the poverty of the worrier. One who wants to know doesn't know anything. He is poor because he worries.

෧෧

9

There will never be love
between men

✤

Jesus said:
Men think, perhaps, that it is peace
which I have come to cast upon the world.
They do not know that it is dissension
which I have come to cast upon the earth:
fire, sword, and war.
For there will be five in a house:
three will be against two, and two against three,
the father against the son, and the son against the father.
And they will stand solitary.

When Jesus says that "there will be five in a house" and they will kill each other he means that there will be no love between men. It is love itself which commits suicide, which has no place in this world. It commits suicide so that no idea of love remains amongst men because there will never be love between them. Indeed that is what Jesus says in the Gospel of Thomas!

No peace, no satisfaction in this world because love, peace or whatever we call That is always prior to the idea we have about it. That doesn't know any definition. But in the world love is defined in all and everything although it can never be defined.

But if we speak of love, if we write about it, it means that at the beginning it is there. In our faraway beginning, it is there.

It is always the love of the Self. And the love of the Self is the knowledge of the Self because in this love there is no more idea of you and me. And no definition of what love is. There is no more the word "love". Of course those are only pointers which never lead anywhere, thanks God!

This is the beauty: "what is" can never be reached: "what is" stays always unreachable and that is freedom. But imagination is always better than Reality: is imagination the beginning of all and does the knowledge of the Self bring more quality? Actually it is totally the opposite: to step out of paradise is wanting to know, it is the desire for knowledge.

The absence of the desire to know is even more than the absence of desire. There is the absence of desire, then the absence of the absence of desire, which is the dissolution of desire. It is a state of non-desire where there is not even the idea of absence of desire. This cannot be reached by a desire because the only thing you can reach is its dissolution or its absence. But the absence of a desire is still its latent presence, the possibility that it reappears. While the absence of the absence is never involved in a desire or a non-desire.

Is it what we call unconditional love?

That doesn't know love.

So the state of love many masters are talking about is a total illusion because it is too late.

Yes, yes, that belongs to this love affair. There is God's love affair with himself, a dream love affair. And the dream is that the lover is different from the beloved. Even unconditional love is conditioned.

This unconditional love is still separation, the separation between conditioned love and unconditioned love. Love never knows conditions or no conditions. It is that what is prior or beyond: no condition nor non-condition, neither personal nor impersonal, because both are ideas which are there only when the lover is there, and the lover will always care, specially about himself. Then he thinks that not caring is better, but not caring is still caring.

It is a dead love. Life which is the Living, never active nor inactive, neither personal nor impersonal, experiences itself in everything that is, but there is no reality in this. Silence is the only reality. The silence without a second is non-duality: That what Brahman is in the absolute non-knowing of himself, in the absolute absence of one who knows or doesn't know. The Absolute lover in the absence of the presence as well as of the absence of a lover.

Any experience is duality. It is the irrelevance of any experience. And its beauty. It is a joy absolutely independent of any presence or absence. If no element of an experience can make you or unmake you, who cares? So the nature of Brahman or of God is carelessness, the absence of the absence of a worrier. This is called unknotting the knots of the knot "me", because in that moment the ownership drops.

There is not even the desire to own because we understand that whatever we can understand is not That.

You are this helplessness, you cannot help yourself! Every time you wake up you cannot avoid the experience of being a lover in love with a beloved. You cannot not realize yourself. You cannot avoid waking up to the realization of what you are, again and again, endlessly. You cannot stop knowing yourself as the seer, the seeing and the seen. You are the whole scenery.

So "everything is Him", as Ranjit Maharaj used to say.

Yes. That and That only!

There is no separation whatsoever.

There is separation but by the experience of separation nobody is separated. That never needs the absence of separation, That is, in separation as in non-separation, because That *is* that what is separation, that what is unity and that what is light. For That there is no difference in nature between ignorance, knowledge and knower. The Heart never makes differences.

The Heart is That! In order to be That nothing is required and this is real satisfaction: no understanding, no getting closer, no knowledge or recognition. Everything is there because you are, and you cannot get rid of it because you are That, and the realization is not different from Reality. You are That and you cannot not be it.

But is it not said that God is love? That is what Jesus says in logion 25:

> *Love your brother like your soul,*
> *guard him like the pupil of your eye.*

Yes, God is also love but he is hate as well. So That what is Absolute love doesn't know love, there is simply no definition of love. And without an idea of love there is love, but without name. You are desiring this absence of difference, this absence of a second idea, this absence of definition. You have the nostalgia of this freedom that you always are. And when you are this freedom you see the stupidity of seeking it. But you, you cannot do anything to gain it. That is why we speak of a divine accident. You are totally immobile but not because of immobility.

I was a hidden God and wanted to know myself.

I fell in love with myself and wanted to know what I loved. Hence this passion. In this imaginary life you are so fascinated by yourself that you constantly fall into your own trap. This is the symbol of the Gnosis: the snake is looking at its own tail and – being fascinated by its movement – it thinks that there is a second snake. This is how everything starts. And when it bites its own tail it realizes that there is no second snake, which then disappears. This is what is called compassion.

Tibetans who have been studying the phenomena of death

have written the " Bardo Thödol". Isn't this text an expression of compassion?

No, but it is a wonderful realization of what you are. For what you are this simply makes no difference, it is neither useful nor useless. What you are never looks for usefulness, never asks if it is beneficial or not: it is part of the entertainment.

There is no compassion in any book: you cannot find compassion in a particular place. Only compassion is because compassion *is* in everything that is. With this acceptance, which is God, it has no place or non-place and there is no particular book which can hold more compassion. You can only speak of self-pity, because we cannot speak about compassion. And nobody can have it: it cannot be imprisoned in a book, or in a particular place, or in a particular truth. Compassion is the absolute absence of a second, when there is not even "one": only then is there compassion. And everything else is self-pity.

Jesus spoke way too much.

Certainly not. I would never say that Jesus spoke too much but rather: "Jesus never spoke". How could he have spoken too much? He never said anything. Like Buddha in the "Diamond Sutra": "There never was a Buddha who walked on Earth and never will be. I preached for forty years but I never said a word to anybody". This is Buddha's ultimate teaching. Jesus never walked on this Earth and That what you are either. That what you are never said anything, never too much, never enough.

What is self-pity?

As long as you are a person, you see others. If you pity others, it comes from your self-pity as a person. First dive into yourself and look at others from there. Since you cannot find anybody inside of you, you cannot find others. This way you will see who is pitying who. Because in this absence of "me" there is no more self-pity. And there is compassion because there are no more others.

10
In Self-knowledge only compassion remains

❧

LOGION 11

Jesus said:
This heaven will pass away,
and the one above it will pass away.
The dead are not alive,
and the living will not die.
In the days when you consumed what is dead,
you made it what is alive.
When you come to dwell in the light,
what will you do?
On the day when you were one
you became two.
But when you become two,
what will you do?

A t the moment there are researchers who are interested by the
functioning of the brain, specially by the way beliefs permeate
it. They say that it works like the body in relation to viruses, namely

that religions - for example - are like an epidemic that spreads to the brain.

Yes, that is the interrelation and the interaction of consciousness. This is called the consciousness of karma, a chain of reactions in consciousness. A significant religious act creates something like an echo that fills the entire consciousness. So consciousness is the most stupid thing there is because it believes everything that it creates.

Is the Gnosis a vaccine, doctor?

The Gnosis is what is called the divine accident, the accidental healing. God was hypnotized by his own movement and by the knowledge of the Self he wakes up from this hypnotic state he had put himself under. This is the snake - as we said before – which is looking at the movement of its own tail and takes this movement for a second snake. With the understanding that what moves is not different from the perceiver or that the perceiver and the perceived are One, with the disappearance of any idea of separation, the hypnosis disappears as well. In Knowledge, the snake becomes again what it is.

But if we bite our tail, it hurts!

The moment you bite your own tail you realize that you are not different from what you know. This is compassion, absolute compassion: as you touch something you recognize that it is yourself you are touching. This compassion is where nobody is there to feel compassion for another. In Self-knowledge only compassion remains. It is an endless Self-experience and this is realization.

How could the snake - which is One - believe that its own tail was a second snake?

By a natural spontaneous awakening into the present. The Absolute unmanifested Self wakes up in the "I" of the awareness, the light, the first experience of being. And from this first experience comes the second experience: "I am the conscious being, the knower". And from this knower comes the ignorance. All this makes a trinity.

Is the third one the state of separation?

Yes, it is the world, the separation, but the sense of being is already the separation because it means dependence. To be aware already means to be dependant on awareness, so it is not freedom. Awareness as the first unfolding of the Self is the mirror of it, but this mirror is breaking into consciousness. In the "I am", the second unfolding, there is timeless space, and from this infinite space the present is being created. But this mirror is also hypnosis.

The first sense of being is the first step out of That. It is already an unfolding. It is no more That. Awareness is a state of being awake, and being awake depends on awakening. But That what is absolute doesn't need awakening to be awake.

Only when awareness knows itself as awareness of That does the question "Who am I?" disappear and only That which is absolute remains: that which is the Mystery and cannot be affected or known. But the awareness of That is already a step outside. The moment you take the notion of existence for real you are out of That.

Only when consciousness knows itself as That is there peace. That is why even being "poor in spirit", or being deprived of everything, even the idea of existence, is already a notion of light, a definition, a manifestation of That, but not That which alone is.

Not knowing what you are, not even feeling what you are, because whatever you can taste is not what you are. Even the first taste of awareness, whatever it may be, is not what you are. You are always that what cannot be tasted, that what cannot be known, that in which no notion of existence can be. The first notion of existence is already a reflection.

Does it mean that I am myself when I have no awareness of myself?

Consciousness depends on you but you don't depend on consciousness. You are absolutely independent of any circumstance.

Consciousness is the definition of a circumstance of existence, of a knowledge of existence. But that which is the absolute Self is totally independent from any knowledge or non-knowledge.

The story of the snake should be completed because when it bites its own tail it is poisoning itself and completely disappears.

The snake is immune to its own poison. In the knowledge of yourself you cannot die. Knowledge can never make you what you are. Nothing can make you what you are, not even the knowledge of what you are, because there is nothing to know.

❧

11
The desire to understand is hell

❧

LOGION 37

His disciples said:
When will you become revealed to us
and when shall we see you?
Jesus said:
When you disrobe without being ashamed
and take up your garments
and place them under your feet like little children
and tread on them,
then will you see the son of the living one,
and you will not be afraid.

To fear is like fearing yourself. Jesus said many times: fear not, fear not what you are. But you are afraid because you don't know what you are. To be afraid of what you are is the craziest idea, like the idea that you have to know yourself not to be afraid. And I am here to show you that this crazy idea is a bloody joke.

The deep sleep about which nothing can be said is maybe this state of nakedness, which now is not accessible to me but which is All.

But what you are in deep sleep is here now. That simply wears a coat and a hat. Without this awareness of the deep sleep there would be no consciousness or realization. Be what you are in deep sleep by knowing absolutely nothing of what it is. That doesn't need any knowing or unknowing. Because this one who knows or doesn't know wakes up in the morning and goes back to sleep at night but that what you are in deep sleep doesn't need this one.

In deep sleep the mind is no more active but the body continues to work. What makes it work?

Who is looking at the body at that time? Who cares if it is working or not?

It works automatically without mind.

So what? Like now! Who cares if it is with or without mind? Everything works by itself and not by the mind.

There is a difference between thoughts and consciousness.

No. Thoughts are only an aspect of consciousness. There is no thinker, that's all! Consciousness is the creator of all the thoughts which are rising, they are consciousness in essence. There is no such thing as "my thoughts", there is no mind! And there is no conscious or unconscious mind: there never was a mind, specially not "my mind".

Yet consciousness is not different from the mind. The problem is that you want to create an advantage: more or less consciousness. And this one who can have an advantage by being more conscious has the absolute disadvantage of being dependent on consciousness.

So forget all of this! There is no such thing as more or less consciousness, it is one of its characteristics. In that what is the realization of this Absolute, consciousness is all there is. It is a total functioning but what you are is there even when there is no consciousness. What you are doesn't depend on consciousness but consciousness depends on that what is the Self. Therefore we say: you are That what is freedom itself.

What does that mean to live unconscious of oneself?

There is nobody who lives consciously or unconsciously. Who cares about consciousness or unconsciousness? Who could have an advantage in living consciously? Do you really believe that the absolute Self needs an advantage? What a poor Self it would be if it would depend upon a conscious life! You are limiting the Absolute!

I don't believe anything, I am only trying to understand.

That is rather difficult, you have my total compassion... The desire to understand is hell because it implies that you don't understand. But how could the Self not understand the Self? Impossible! It understands itself in understanding as well as in non-understanding. It never needs a special circumstance of understanding to be what it is. What a weird idea! On the other hand I will tell you to try to understand even harder, even if it doesn't make any difference, because you cannot do otherwise. And trying not to try makes it even more difficult. There is no way out of it!

As long as you have a hope you are in hell. In German, there is an expression to say "being pregnant": *in guter Hoffnung sein,* to be in good hope. You are pregnant with the idea that one day you will know yourself. It is very pregnant! "If I only could know myself one day I would be more what I am".

You are pregnant but you never give birth.

There is no delivery, no childbirth, because you don't reach what you are through understanding. And the understanding which appeared will disappear, that is for sure. We can only talk about this understanding which is your nature - which never appears nor disappears - by being That what is absolute. And being That is the absolute understanding, without one who understand or not.

I can have the illusion that the illusion is no more there.

Beautiful idea! But when there is no more the idea of "no idea" it is an indication of this nakedness Jesus speaks about, of that which is prior and defines nothing. It is never a definition but the total absence of any idea or non-idea. No indication, you have no information whatsoever. In this way there is no attachment nor non-attachment.

Sometimes I have the feeling that the illusion, the worries, are like a cloud that is separating me from the Self and I only have to wait for the cloud to vanish. Am I wrong?

It is not a mistake but you are looking from this side of the clouds. For the sun it is always sunny. When you are that what is prior you are like the sun, which doesn't worry about the clouds. But as long as there is someone who sees clouds there are clouds, or absence of clouds. The sun never sees clouds, it shines, that's all. In a famous story of the Upanishads, the night goes to God and complains: "Every morning I must go when the sun rises. It is killing me!" God asks the sun: "Who are you to kill the night in this way?" And the sun answers: "Which night?"

Like the sun, when you are what you are you never know anything. You are, that's all, you are this Absolute light, which simply shines without knowing on what it shines. Many cultures have chosen the sun as a God - such as the Mayas - because the sun doesn't make any distinction, it merely shines. And That, you are!

The rising of the inner sun, the rising of awareness is the rising of this unpredictable sun which cannot be forced, nor created, nor controlled. No matter how hard you try you cannot do anything to make it rise or prevent it to rise. It rises when it rises but not "because". To see that you cannot do anything is already peace because then there is no action nor free will. It is a foretaste.

Although we have realized that intelligence doesn't lead to the vision of the real, how come you keep calling upon our intelligence through explanations or perfectly convincing analogies like the story of the sun? At the same time if it doesn't go through my intelligence, nothing works.

Nothing will work, that is the beauty! And nothing needs to work for what you are. I am calling upon your Absolute intelligence, upon That what is the sun, by knowing nothing, by giving up all relative knowledge, by becoming That what is Knowledge itself, the intelligence which shines eternally, which is the Absolute Self, like the Holy Spirit. No "me" has this intelligence: it is pure intelligence as Absolute consciousness. And That speaks, and That listens. It is not "my" or "your" intelligence. I never call upon your intelligence. I am speaking to what I am.

We are terribly thirsty for Being. We are in a state of expectancy.

You are like horses. I can bring you to the water but I cannot make you drink. You are thirsty and that is why you are here. So I don't need to take you anywhere. You will drink by yourself.

This is a direct appointment with what you are. And nobody can avoid it and nothing is required for it, no preparation. We can never be prepared for what we are. And this idea of being better prepared than another is just the arrogance of the seeker.

We try to explain, to understand. Where we function as human beings, what we are in reality remains totally unknown to us, totally mysterious. Such is the functioning inside consciousness. It needs a mental adjustment which is not so easy for us.

No. You are played by consciousness as perfectly as you can be. No problem. You are played by this Absolute consciousness which plays ignorant for sheer entertainment.

But why does this perfect unpronounceable Absolute consciousness enjoy playing ignorant?

Because ignorance is as perfect as knowledge. It is a point of view without point.

❧

12

If you want to come to me
you have to be naked

❧

LOGION 54

Jesus said:
Blessed are the poor,
for yours is the kingdom of heaven.

No "owner" will ever reach that what is heaven, the paradise. Therefore Jesus said: If you want to come to me you have to be naked [1]. In the non-definition of God there is only God. In the non-definition of truth there is only truth. But nobody can own the truth.

(1) "Blessed are the poor in spirit, for theirs is the kingdom of heaven" (Matthew 5:3).

What you say is totally in accordance with logion 78:

Jesus said:
Why have you come out into the desert?
To see a reed shaken by the wind?
And to see a man clothed in fine garments

like your kings and your great men?
Upon them are the fine garments,
and they are unable to discern the truth.

The stripping of ideas is the owner's or the doer's great departure. Let the ships reach the open sea by seeing that it is a dropping of the mind. Ramana Maharshi said: Only one thing is keeping you from what you are: the idea of "me". Drop this possession. Then you will be perfect as you ever were.

I am in the unknowing of myself and the lightning bolt, which makes me become conscious of myself is very fleeting.

But what I am is eternally present. I always go back to this pure perception. That is always what is, first and last, and That doesn't need any consciousness. Consciousness is a phantom who appears in perception but this perception is never affected, never changed by any flesh or whatever you can name. This innocence cannot penetrate any meaning. This consciousness having an experience, and the experience itself, are merely shadows. So consciousness is of no help: in this sense consciousness itself needs help.

Consciousness is a dreamer who dreams. And this dream of consciousness appears in this pure perception which is the eye of God and cannot be stained. It is always That which is the "groundless ground" Master Eckhart was talking about, That which never needs a ground, nor a knowledge, nor anything.

What happens when a person is overwhelmed by depression?

For this separate person who always needs a meaning in life, existence becomes empty of all sense. And it is unbearable. But for what you are, this lightness, this absence of sense is pure joy. But for one who is separate this happiness is unbearable because he cannot stay separate. And he is afraid. This idea of being born is so strong that the fear of death comes with it. As long as birth is a reality you fear this infinite, because you don't know. When you see that this Unborn is your nature then there is nothing to carry or to bear.

Nobody can bear this lightness. "The unbearable lightness of Being". It depresses you because you are in the void, this void which will teach you and empty you so that you become the void of the void. Because only the void of the void doesn't know the void. The Buddhists, who are very concerned by Emptiness, say that Emptiness is the only teacher. Then you become accustomed to the void, which will erase you at the end. What is in the void cannot remain. At the beginning you do everything to avoid it until you cannot do it anymore. Then it devours you. And when you are no more there, the void is no more.

The Buddhists also say that "samsara is nirvana and nirvana is samsara". Does that mean that it is pointless to look for nirvana because it is already here now anyway, samsara being the world where we are?

You cannot look for nirvana because you are nirvana. It always goes this way: God is looking for God with the idea that God must know what is God and wants to make God a place. So he really has a problem.

Is this why only the Self can choose the Self?

No. For that what is the Self there is no choice. There is an absence of choice. The Almighty has no power because there is no second that the first could control. The Self cannot even control himself. Absolute helplessness!

So God is not the Almighty but totally powerless?

He is almighty because there is no second which can control him. But he never can control himself because for control you need two. Since God is all there is there is absolutely no control. The controller cannot control the controller. Therefore it is the Almighty without a necessity of control. Absolute power is simply to be That!

To be alone.

You will never be able to bear being alone. Never. And nobody can stay alone because in this solitude without a second the very idea of being alone is not there. Not even "one" remains. Because for the idea of one you need two. This is why it is called Advaita, non-duality.

It is before the words and prior to consciousness.

Prior. Beyond the beyond, which is prior. You get lost in the beyond.

H.W.L. Poonja said: "Beyond the words you are, be simply that".

I will add... "because you cannot be otherwise". For That you don't need to do anything, not even to be beyond, which can still be a desire. But you are what you are with desire or without desire. Whether you are stupid or intelligent you cannot lose this absolute knowledge, because you are That, whether you like it or not. You play stupid, that's all.

Everyone is playing stupid!

No. There is only one who is stupid, the Self! And I think he endlessly enjoys the stupidity. So be That what always enjoys, That what is happiness itself and cannot help being happy. Even if it tries to avoid happiness it cannot, because avoiding is still happiness itself, it is unavoidable.

Did you really say that my nature is happiness itself?

Yes, your nature is the absence of one who is happy or unhappy. And this is pure happiness.

13
Everything is a bridge which leads nowhere

ొ

LOGION 45

Jesus said:
Grapes are not harvested from thorns,
nor are figs gathered from thistles,
for they do not produce fruit...

H*ow to live life or to be lived by life in the best possible way?*

There is no such thing as "living life". What is living what?

How to live a pure life?

What is a pure life? A pure life is the dirtiest idea I know because if you speak of a pure life there is an impure life as well. So the very idea of a pure life is stained. There is nobody who lives life or is lived by life. Who wants to know? Who needs to know what Life is? Who wants to control it? "Me"! Starting from what? Starting from the existential crisis of a "me", a spirit, a phantom.

A phantom wants to know Life and to become himself the Living.

The beauty of Life is that it cannot be known or controlled by a phantom or by anything. This little "me", this idea, wants to control Life, but thanks God, Life cannot be controlled by anyone, known or unknown. Again whatever we can know or understand only relates to this relative life and has no meaning for the Life that you are.

The river doesn't care whether the fish goes upstream or downstream.

The fish thinks that it exists. An idea thinks that an idea exists. There again it is the root thought "I" which always wants to know: it is already a phantom and the phantom needs to understand. He always needs something. He needs a second: without a second he cannot survive. A phantom needs a reflection because he himself is already a reflection, so he ponders on what is life. Sometimes he thinks he has found a solution: "I go with the flow!" This idea sounds good until he comes to a waterfall!

In this sense we are coming back to logion 19: "Blessed is he who came into being before he came into being".

Yes, and I am speaking to That. This is why I call those talks "Self-talks". I don't want to provide any help. I can only point out that there is never the slightest necessity for That what is prior to existence. Only there is the peace that is never disrupted by understanding, misunderstanding or any other blah-blah, interesting or not. Everybody here has an intense desire for this peace. And I can only take away what can be taken away.

LOGION 40

Jesus said:
A grapevine has been planted outside of the father,
but being unsound,
it will be pulled up by its roots and destroyed.

What you are will always be the absolute left over, the absolute substratum from which nothing more can be subtracted. And this is peace itself without knowing it, by being it. I always say: know yourself as you know yourself in deep deep sleep.

Is it in deep sleep that we are most awake?

There is nobody who *is* awake, neither here nor in deep sleep. In deep sleep there is only awareness and nobody who is aware. That is the main point: in awareness there is no one because there is no time, no second. So everything that comes from this idea of a second, this idea of being born, is a concept that we adopt.

Isn't the "I am", the feeling of existing, a bridge toward the ultimate Reality?

As you see the bridge, you see that you are not the bridge. At the end it comes down to seeing that whatever you experience, even the experiencer, belongs to the experience and is not what you are. Everything is a bridge which leads nowhere. Infinite bridges but none to cross. Therefore H.W.L Poonja said: "Be quiet". Don't follow any shadow because even consciousness is a shadow. Consciousness needs you but you never need consciousness.

What you are suggesting is to change our point of view.

To drop all points of view. It is a point without a point.

Isn't it better to have a beautiful dream versus a nightmare?

For what you are it doesn't make any difference. That knows no dream nor dreamer. And what makes a difference is not what you are. You are this acceptance, you are the source of heaven and hell, and the source makes no difference between the two. You are the absolute Self.

As long as we see others there is "one". And when you start from this one there is self-pity. This little self needs help in one way or another because he doesn't know himself. To know oneself is not to know any other. You don't know yourself, how can you know what others are? So look for the void just like the void is looking for you, because the void is unavoidable!

How can I look for the void if I am the void?

By not fearing it because you are the void. This is the only true way of looking for it. To recognize yourself in That what is the void is Self-knowledge. Thus you don't fear it any more.

(1) "So have no fear of them, for nothing is covered that will not be revealed, or hidden that will not be known." (Matthew 10:26). " There is no fear in love." (John 4:18).

What you call pure perception, is it the perception of the void?

It is like a void. A void of ideas, a void of forms and even of non-form. It is the emptiness of this awareness, like a flow. The total absence of "me" or of any idea, because any idea is an appearance. But not That: That never comes or goes. It is always first and last.

Would you say that in this pure perception phantoms of forms and thoughts simply appear as phantoms or they don't appear at all?

Never mind if they appear or not. When you are that what is emptiness, who cares if they appear or not, if they remain or not? Only a shadow cares about a shadow. The void doesn't care about it. It doesn't even care about not caring about it. And this one who cares still belongs to fleeting appearances.

When you look at me, what do you see?

I see a form of myself.

So who is this fleeting shadow?

The form is fleeting but not That what I am. The form is simply a dream form but That what is the form never comes or goes. It is totally immobile. So I never speak to those fleeting forms which appear as a mother, a daughter, etc. I see them but they are only "pfft!" because I always speak to That what is unborn and never dies and not to something conditioned by circumstances, something which is only a vibration in consciousness. It is there and it is not there. Always this paradox, I see it and I don't see it.

Would you say that these appearing forms have a seeming existence only because you are?

No. That what is Existence is unchanging and only That is. The rest has no existence.

And who is dreaming?

The dreamer belongs to this fleetingness, it appears in the morning and goes at night. And this Unknown which is prior to the dream, which is what we may call the Absolute dreamer, which never moves, never leaves what it is, this Dreamer who never needs that a dream or a dreamer disappears or appears, is Life itself, the Living! The rest is dead.

But this fear, that prevents me from letting myself be erased by the void, has it been created by the dreamer? Is the fear of losing myself an obstacle?

This fear is the idea of an owner, "my self". You are really afraid to lose this self that you call "yours". And because of this dream idea, you lost yourself! All I can do is to repeat that you cannot lose what you are. This fear is but a phantom who is afraid of That what is the phantom, because by being That what is the phantom, the phantom disappears. One of the survival systems of this problem "me" is never being able to accept that there is no problem. This is what it fears most, this is its biggest problem, because without problems it cannot exist. Therefore it is never short of problems.

If the Self doesn't need anything why all this game of the manifestation, this game of ignorance? Unless it makes absolutely no difference for the Self?

There are infinite differences but they make no difference. This moment is unique, it resembles no other moment. For what you are there is always oneness without any comparison. Universe, oneness. The difference is Absolute, because it doesn't make any difference. It is an absolute difference for that what makes a difference.

The Absolute advantage is the absolute absence of one who can have an advantage or a disadvantage: it is an absolute advantage but this Absolute doesn't know this advantage. So this absolute Knowledge is there even in what we call ignorance. That what is Knowledge itself becomes a form of relative knowledge and a form of ignorance. But it is always the Absolute Knowledge. In essence both ignorance and the relative knowledge are the Absolute knowledge. There is only this Absolute knowledge of the Self in whatever circumstances and in whatever forms. Only the Self is, that is what matters! The rest is a definer who defines without defining anything.

14

A form can never become That what is the form

৵৬

Jesus said:
If the flesh came into being because of spirit,
it is a wonder.
But if spirit came into being because of the body,
it is a wonder of wonders.
Indeed, I am amazed at how this great wealth
has made its home in this poverty.

We have been talking a lot about the mind but it appears to me that, through my body, there is a tiny possibility to know what energy is, what Chinese call Ki.

We can only know energy through its effects and not directly because we are energy. And if we are energy there is no experience nor experiencer. The energy that we can know is only its reflection and not the energy itself. So the direct experience of the Self is to be what is. There is only the absolute experience of the Self and not relative experiences experienced by individuals. There are only effects and That what gives rise to them cannot be perceived.

The body is a means, the body is a statement.

The body is the effect of an information but consciousness can be perceived only as information, never as consciousness. That what is without form cannot be perceived and the form is but the effect of That what has no form. Same thing with energy: it has no form and can never be directly perceived as energy, only as effect. But who is interested in what can be lost again? Whatever you find is already lost the moment you find it, because it is in time.

The center which is trying to know doesn't exist.

Yes, like in Ramana Maharshi's meditation "Who am I?": the meditator meditates directly on the meditator. It is not a meditation directed towards a goal because the question "Who am I?" indicates that the meditator himself is the Absolute. With this question the source asks directly the question to itself, awareness focuses on itself, on That what it is. "Who am I?" is an infinite enquiry of the Self.

By starting from "am I", first we look outside, then we turn to ourselves with "Who", straight on the meditator. So it is directly meditating on the meditator himself, on That what is the essence of the meditator. Then... there is the Mystery. Buddha said: "The eye cannot see the eye" and whatever the eye can see cannot be the eye. You are That what is the eye. You are prior to experience and experiencing, and this is the eye of God.

Does the body have a role to play in the realization?

Not in the realization itself but - according to numerous saints - the energy is modified in the body after the realization of the awareness of the Absolute. By becoming aware of its essence, each cell goes through experiences of heat and light but always in accordance with the body. It is a side-effect, it is not important.

But in the process of realization the body is neither a tool nor an obstacle, it doesn't play any role.

Nevertheless it will feel the effects. Because at that point the energy cannot be controlled by an "I". In Hindi it is called *kundalini,* a free flow of energy. And when the power of this snake wakes up you cannot stay still in front of this beast, which is consciousness. Because in this compassion everything that is perceived is a direct experience of the energy in all its different vibrations, without filter or defence. Without a way out.

So the body has become a fuse transmitting energy, and this energy can illuminate the whole world from there.

It is a vibratory field. Usually there is an armour around you, a filtration system that lets in what you want and pushes away what you don't want. But with this compassion everything is open. And this can make one paranoiac because it has no explanation. Sometimes people find themselves in a psychiatric hospital. For them it is unbearable. The armour breaks and this energy rises without filtering emotions or information, without any filtration system.

Does Karl agree with the Hindu tradition that the physical body is a reflection, a materialisation of a subtle body, that this energy circulates through canals called nadis or meridians, and the meeting points between the physical body and the subtle body are the chakras?

Yes, the endocrine glands are indeed chakras. As you know, the thymus gland starts shrinking and closes at about fourteen years. But when this realization happens and the controller dies, the *kundalini* circulates freely and the energy becomes a circle again. When the circle is complete, you become space-like and this is unbearable for the "me" because it erases completely the idea of separation. And if this doesn't happen at the right moment it will be taken as a mental disease. But there is nothing to fear from those extraordinary experiences of light, it is perfectly natural.

Only when this idea of separation vanishes you become That what is consciousness itself. Then there is nobody who is crazy or not: you are what you are at all levels. Nothing to fear, and when there is no fear there is no problem. This fear is there only when you don't understand what is happening to you: you come out of limitation and enter into something that is not different from what you are. So in a way you regain what you already are. To fear what you are is completely crazy. When you see that there is nothing left but what you are, you simply are in this peace. And this energy makes no difference.

After having had such experiences many people come to see me in order to maintain a kind of equilibrium by understanding what triggers this energy. Because this stillness is not dead. It is pure energy, as if 100 000 volts were circulating through a narrow canal. It is very delicate! When fear is no more there, blocks and resistances can dissolve because the opening happens through acceptance, and the energy can only circulate freely when the opening is total. Then you are this energy. To fear it is simply crazy. This is why Jesus says: Fear not what you are, because to fear what you are is ignorance. By knowing you are That, there is nothing to fear. So no resistance.

When this compassion happens resistance is futile. It will take you anyway, whether you like it or not. When Grace is after you it is merciless. You can never be ready to receive it. Simply see that this Grace is not different from what you are.

Is this what is called a dissociation of the personality?

It is the erasing of the idea of "me" and "mine", the idea of ownership. Without ownership, no need for defences. Therefore I first say: you are not the body, you are not this or that, so that this idea of possession disappears. And without possession, no need for a defence system. And without a defence system, no resistance.

It is different from the dissociation of the personality when those who can no more function in this world are locked in or put to sleep in a chemical straightjacket, but in what Karl says, I think that something of the person remains, which enables him or her to exist in this world.

I am not interested in a person who has to function in the world. If there is any interest, it is that the person disappears. I am this merciless Grace which has no need to be held under control. Functioning in this society is a dream which takes place in another dream. Whether this functioning happens or not makes no difference.

And what becomes of this body?

What it always was: energy. Before there was only energy and after there will be energy only. When energy takes the form of this body it remains energy: an information of energy, that's all. And when this form turns into another one, no danger because there is no such thing as "my" body or "my" life or "my" functioning in a so-called society, so nothing to defend. It totally works by itself and never because of a so-called control. It always was this way and always will be. The controller is a phantom who never controlled anything. And to make it more sane is a really insane idea.

Nisargadatta said: "Everything is predetermined. Everything you do, the big like the small things, and even what I am saying now, everything is predetermined. I don't even care about it."

Yes, he was right because in the manifestation of what you are there is no coming and going. That what is the realization is as infinite as you are. Nothing comes and nothing goes. And since the future is already there and the past also, what to do? If everything is already done, what is there to do and for whom?

We must become aware that everything is done. That's all. After we drop...

Even if there is nothing to drop... You drop that you cannot drop. You give up what you never had. You give up the dropper. You renounce the renouncer. And this can only be done by Grace. Grace renounces the renunciation.

You will find, that is certain, but you don't know when. And you will find that there is nothing to find. At the end emptiness will always be there. And since you are the substratum which is even in the void That what is the void, there will be a point of void. And in this void you will experience that this experience cannot change what you are. It is the experience of death, the experience of the void in the absence of the world and of time, and even in this absolute circumstance you are.

And what happens when the body is involved in an accident?

At the moment of an accident the physical pain is sometimes so violent than the Spirit detaches itself from the body and seems to witness events from space. When the pain is unbearable it detaches itself from the form as if it was programmed. And often in meditation, when the search becomes unbearable, one detaches oneself from the world and turn to That what is the Spirit.

But this happens also whenever you go to sleep and then it is quite natural. The only goal of meditation is to experience this sleep in waking state, meaning to be awake with this perception of absence of ego, when the Spirit is turned to itself.

Isn't meditation an escape?

You cannot not meditate because everything is meditation. Sometimes the attention is directed outside and sometimes it is directed inside, but in both cases it is not you who decides on the direction. Whether you look outside by meditating on the information or you look inside, towards the space-like Spirit, in both cases it is always consciousness that meditates on what it is. So every action, personal or impersonal, is an action of consciousness directed towards itself. When there is meditation you are That what is meditation, so you are the Totality meditating on the Totality in all its possible or impossible forms, outside like inside. By not finding yourself outside nor inside you are That what is the absolute seeker who will never be able to find himself. But nothing stops, consciousness will always be in meditation.

Karl, you say: "Be what you are". Before you say this sentence, I am That. When you say it, I am That and after, I am still That. What do those words bring me?

It brings you the confidence that what you are doesn't change. You are That before, during and after. And nothing is happening. It is Joy rejoicing in the changes, given that nothing changes in changes. And this, *ad infinitum.* "Meditation" is just another word for an absolute action of Totality which is without intention because by an action of Totality nothing changes. So everything is meditation.

It may be what Jesus meant in this logion when he said about the spirit and the body: "...it is a wonder".

Yes, then everything is a wonder, moment by moment, the wonder of Being in itself. Actually this is what Zen is: the next sip of coffee, or whatever comes, is an absolute realization of Being. An infinite wonder.

Why did Jesus say: "Indeed, I am amazed at how this great wealth has made its home in this poverty"?

Once Ramana Maharshi was asked why his body was shaking. His answered: " If an elephant enters a weak hut, what will happen to the body? [1]". In this image the elephant represents the cosmic consciousness imprisoned in the restricting container of the body. It is the Holy Spirit of the Christians which found itself in this body, meaning which put itself in something limited. But it is not that some being came into another one! Same with the Spirit which dwells in the body. How could it enter this vehicle? Why? That is always the question, it is a wonder! Like some self-proclaimed saints in India, to the question "Why?", we can as well answer "Why not?".

(1) *Living by the Words of Bhagavan, David Godman.*

Isn't it as if the manifestation would sometimes allow us, as individuals, to feel through the body something like a perception of what we are?

No, the body is just another form of perception, which also belongs to imagination. And a form can never become That what is the form. If a form becomes more open or more vast this is only a matter of quantity: what was limited before is no more limited. But both aspects belong to imagination because without that what is narrow, nothing can be vast and vice versa. It is the polarization of the realization. Both aspects belong to imagination but this one who imagines all of this is neither one nor the other. He is never tight in tightness or at ease in vastness. And what is tight in tightness or at ease in vastness is the first ego-consciousness. Consciousness being tight or at ease always depends on this first imagination, so it is already imaginary. One who defines himself as this or that is already a definition, what comes down to say that you will never perceive yourself in differences but in That what is prior to the difference, where there is no experience.

When the "elephant enters a hut", as Ramana Maharshi said, isn't it an ordeal that it imposes on itself?

No, it has no choice. It is Being in its freedom. What to do? You have to be what you are in tightness as in vastness otherwise it wouldn't be worth being it.

Reality doesn't need words but an individual needs them. That is probably why Jesus talks in this way in this logion. But isn't it only in appearance that we separate a thing from another?

Yes, there is the experience of separation but the experience of separation has no reality. It is the dream of the experience of being born in birth and therefore to become somebody born, it is the experience of mortality. From the first false idea comes a second false idea, and so on.

But we need to be informed of our true nature. Doesn't Jesus say in logion 21: "Let there be among you a man of understanding".

You don't have to be informed because in reality you didn't get lost in the experience. Reality never gets lost in the experience of the non-real. Thus we cannot reach Reality by an experience of the non-real.

But the silent Spirit carries in itself a kind of energy. We feel it, it is tangible.

It is still the feeling of "I am", which is not separate. The unitary Spirit, or Holy Spirit, is the nature of all of you here, but experienced individually by each one. Silence and movement are not separate, they are two different ways of experiencing energy. They are the two main poles. Of course the unitary Spirit will always favour the absence of suffering while in the separate spirit there is the pain of separation that we always try to transcend.

Before the separate spirit and the unitary Spirit there is the light of awareness of the Father. It is the highest level of consciousness, the beginning and the end of what can be experienced. God as such perceives himself in the form of the purest light. Then, in the second experience he perceives himself as "I am", the Spirit. And in the third experience, he perceives himself as human. All of this can be experienced but That is never perceived as such.

So light is already second hand. Because God's nature is before and beyond the light. Reality is before the realization of the realizer, before the realization of the Spirit and before the realization of the light. This trinity in itself is the Heart. And the Heart will never recognize itself as such. Heart knows itself as the Father, as the Spirit and as the Son.

Jesus said in logion 77: "It is I who am the light which is above them all".

Yes, be a light upon yourself. It is the first and the last experience. God starts where that what can be experienced stops. And where the experience starts God stops. It is very simple. Where the knower starts Knowledge stops. We cannot find peace in whatever experience and this is also mentioned in the Gospel of Thomas.

Yes, in logion 27: "If you do not fast as regards the world, you will not find the kingdom".

This is the peace which is the nature of what is but can never be felt, the joy of That what cannot be known. So the worst we can imagine, that there will never be peace, is joy! There will never be peace for anybody – it is unattainable, and this is joy!

❧

15

In spite of the madness of ideas you are what you are

❦

The disciples said to Jesus:
Tell us how our end will be.
Jesus said:
Have you discovered, then, the beginning,
that you look for the end?
For where the beginning is,
there will the end be.
Blessed is he who will take his place in the beginning;
he will know the end
and will not experience death.

Jesus talks to That what is prior. And That what is prior to the beginning is also prior to the end. The prior is beyond and the beyond is prior. Nisargadatta talked about That what is prior to consciousness, it is also the title of one of his books: "Prior to consciousness". Be the beginning and you will be the end.

What you are is not an object of sensation. You are not an object. You are not in this world, you are not of this world. You are always prior, and never in anything.

Whatever I say about myself, I am always prior.

Yes, always prior. Prior to everything. You are always prior to the world, prior to the senses, prior to whatever you can imagine. But to be able to think you must be, and this is what you are. This is Knowledge, the knowledge of the Self: to be prior to knowledge. This is why we call That the substratum from which nothing more can be subtracted, where nothing more is prior. It is the *Urgrund* Master Eckhart was talking about: "The groundless ground". The base, which has no more base.

Logion 84 refers to models, which were in us at the beginning:
Jesus said:
When you see your likeness,
you rejoice.
But when you see your images
which came into being before you,
and which neither die nor become manifest,
how much you will have to bear!

This means that the infinite of Existence is unbearable for the relative ego because the little "I" can never grasp the extent, the immensity of the infinite, and in this unbearable state he disappears. Only this infinite state is the lightness of Being. "The unbearable Lightness of Being" is well described in this logion. Because for That which is prior to everything this lightness is natural. But for one who is only an image of it That is unbearable and stays unattainable. The idea of "Being" can never become That what is prior to the idea. Whatever this idea does to attain That what is prior to it remains an idea. It is the futility of any desire, any action, any effort to become what we are. No action, no knowledge can make you what you are. The image can never become what it represents. An idea never becomes That where it comes from. It is dead. Any idea is dead. Life itself is prior to any idea of life. And That what is not an idea of life, that what is Life itself doesn't know Life because it *is* Life.

I am real Life. I am not something alive, I am the Living itself. The prior is unthinkable and that is why you are the unthinkable. You cannot think before you think. Whatever is said or not comes always after. So I cannot pre-think myself. I am always before the idea. Thinking is a reflection and not a pre-reflection.

If I say, "me, the Absolute", it is too late because there has been a recognition. I cannot say that.

Whether you say it or not, whether you think it or not, whether you know it or not, is irrelevant. You *are* it anyway. It is freedom, or peace. Free from all necessity to know yourself or not.

Is joy the nature of Nature, is it happiness, but happiness without object and which doesn't cling to anything outside?

Nature without somebody joyful. Without circumstances of joy. This is why it is called silence. Personal happiness depends on relative harmony. You call absence of suffering being happy or satisfied. But how much more intense or real is happiness without one who can be happy or miserable! The absence of a sufferer is the silence you are, which never depends on anybody suffering or being happy.

Isn't the illusory presence of this person the very root of suffering?

The root thought of the sufferer is the falling in love with himself. This love story is suffering.

Is this what happens soon after birth?

Even before birth. It is falling in love with the first light, the first notion of existence.

It is what starts to limit what was unlimited.

No, it creates duality. In this very first light with which you fall in love, there is already two "me's": the subtlest me and myself. With the first notion of existence there is two. This is what Buddha called the accident. The first imagination.

I think this is what Jesus meant when he talked about unveiling the beginning.

Yes, the beginning and the end. Because the beginning is the end of illusion. If you see the beginning as the first notion you see that this first notion is already a phantom who cannot be what you are. And in this, you rest. Because you cannot know more than the light.

The French writer Céline was nothing of a Gnostic but he understood that: from birth on, what was to come was going to be totally catastrophic. He said in a humourous way that the first mistake had been to be born.

That's what I say: it is a crazy idea and from this first crazy idea of soul and psyche the mental hospital starts.

But there is no mistake.

That is not the question. Every aspect of existence is an absolute aspect of existence but what I am talking about is: how to know oneself? And as soon as you know yourself as something born, as soon as you take this body for "your body" and see it as different and separate from another body, most probably it is not going to be enjoyable. At the moment of separation nothing works anymore. But when you know yourself as That about which God says: "I am That I am", everything is fine in this world. To know yourself as That without knowing what you are or what you are not is a pointer of this happiness without second.

Where is the place of consciousness in all this?

We can say that consciousness is the realization of That.

Then there is two.

No, no, there is no two. The non-manifested or potential

existence and consciousness as realization of That are not different. They are One in essence. So you can say that there is Reality, the potential existence, and consciousness is the realization of it: potential or awake, both are what is because there is no two. So potential or awake, there is no two.

I am exactly what I am.

The beauty is that you can say whatever you want, everybody can say whatever they want, in spite of whatever is said or thought, the nature of everyone here is That what is God himself. In spite of the madness of ideas you are what you are. Whether you are very intelligent or very precise or whatever, it makes no difference. So don't worry, it is irrelevant.

"Simply be quiet and see what happens", H.W.L. Poonja said.

Whether you speak or not you always remain what you are. H.W.L. Poonja may have said "Be quiet and see" but That doesn't need to be quiet because That never said anything. And what can be quiet is never quiet enough. With or without words, That what is your nature never said a single word and will never go out of itself. In spite of the words, in spite of this quietness we can speak of, you are silence. So don't worry and be happy. For me this is the nature and the beauty of Existence. Always in spite of. You can create infinite concepts and it makes no difference. You can also create a new concept to stop all concepts but whatever solution you come up with, there will always be: and then, and then, and then… In spite of all of this, you are. The nature of your Absolute existence never depends upon whether you know it or not. Knowledge is absolutely independent from whoever knows or doesn't know.

It always remains a distance, a blindness, a mystery.

But those are only words! The base of Ramakrishna's teachings was simple: to be able to doubt Existence first you must exist, that's all.

Even the infinite needs a definer. Whether I say "I am" or "I am the body" both need this first "I". And this one is already a phantom. The phantom in "I am" is infinite and in this body it is finite. So there is an infinite phantom and a finite phantom. Poor phantom… This is why we speak of this non-knowledge prior to this first "I". This is called peace. Even the idea of infinite – as we said – is unbearable.

We must wake up from our sleep to be aware of our sleep.

The Buddhists call this "the wall of perception" because the perceiver is the last light, then there is total unknowing. The first imagination is the light and you cannot go beyond.

Everything comes spontaneously but it has no name.

This is again the phantom. The idea of spontaneity or non-spontaneity needs him. For the Absolute there is not even spontaneity. Because for That nothing ever happened. Whatever you say depends on this first phantom. Without him there is neither imagination nor spontaneity. Spontaneity or not both depend on him. Those notions are not false *per se* but they depend on the imaginary world of this phantom. And your nostalgia is the desire of That, namely consciousness, and it is endless. If, in a split second, you can see that it will never end, surprise, there never was a beginning.

16
God's love story or the ultimate sex

❧

LOGION 22

Jesus said to them:
When you make the two one,
and when you make the inside like the outside
and the outside like the inside,
and the above like the below,
and when you make the male and the female
one and the same,
so that the male not be male
nor the female female...
then will you enter the kingdom.

For the Hebrews the first man is Adam and Eve is the first woman. Eve is the "I am", it is already life. The world rises from the union of Adam and Eve. God himself, Nature, became male and female, and from this love story the world is born. In India they say that it is God's love story or the ultimate sex: Shiva becomes intelligent and the *lingam* penetrates the *yoni*, the "I am". Truth penetrates truth in imagination and the whole universe appears. In That there is an absolute potential from which everything you can imagine rises: the first male, the first female, but it is always an imaginary Creation.

I think this logion is advice to avoid getting locked up in a masculine or a feminine identity, which identifies with a person. This has nothing to do with a specific sex.

Buddha could have said: be undecided. It is the middle way, neither man nor woman. But don't create a mixture to get something new. No, simply be as you are, neither man nor woman nor anything you can imagine, always undecided, neither this nor that, always *neti-neti*. Being undecided means: "Be quiet". Don't move towards this or that. It is not even walking in the middle way but simply: "Be as you are". You are not what you can imagine because this is fleeting, as any idea is.

Ramana Maharshi said that the only suicide you can commit is to think that you are born, to take yourself for a relative object. From this point there are only mistakes. The root of the mistake is the idea that you exist, and any idea that results from this is a mistake. Whatever we can say about ourselves comes from this root idea "I". It always starts with this phantom and whatever he does depends on him.

The beauty of your existence is that there never was a necessity that anything appears, disappears or changes to be what you are. But I can only point this out to you. You have to be what you are without any doubt like in deep sleep. This one who wakes up in the morning, sometimes doubting and sometimes not, sometimes understanding and sometimes not, is anyway a phantom, but your existence was never depending on him. So know yourself as you know yourself in deep sleep by being totally independent from one who knows or not in order to exist or not. Because only this existence is the knowledge which never needs a knower or a non-knower, never needs a form of knowledge or non-knowledge. So be "in spite of" and never "because". But we can also talk about it, no harm.

What is the difference between deep sleep and what Hindus call OM?

OM is the first sound, what is called the Word in the Gospels. Om is the first light. Buddha said: "Be a light upon yourself", meaning: Be That what is the light but doesn't know the light. The first light that you know cannot be the light that you are. Be yourself a light doesn't mean that the first experience of light is what you are. You are That what is the light. The first light that you can experience is already an imagination. Om, this first sound and this first light, is the first presence of your existence, the first presence that you can experience, but it is not what you are in essence. It is not different but it is already being aware, it is awareness.

But you are not awareness, you are That what is awareness, then you are That what is the "I am", then you are That what is the world. But you are not the world, you are not the "I am" and you are not the "I". Jesus said: I am the Father but I am not the Father, I am the Holy Spirit but I am not the Holy Spirit and I am the man but I am not the man, I am that what is That. This is pointing out the absolute ground of Existence, which itself is groundless. But the first base is the light, OM, the beginning of the circus. You can say that you are the absolute source of it, but for you there is no source.

(1) "In the beginning was the Word, and the Word was with God, and the Word was God", The Prologue of the Gospel of John.

Even this is in only a pointer, thanks God, it doesn't help because God never needs help or pointers. Everyone here came to receive the most precious gift: nothing can be given to you that you are not already.

In the analogy of the deep sleep there can be no doubt. But there can be no certainty either.

It is a total independence from the certainties nobody needs. It is the absence of somebody, of "me" or "no me", the absence of a phantom, therefore of any necessity whatsoever. It simply indicates: Know yourself as That what is Knowledge itself, in spite of this first ignorant phantom who sometimes thinks that he knows. But an imagination imagining that it knows or doesn't know is still an imagination. No matter how profound, this depth can only be imaginary, whatever this phantom says, including this one *(Karl points at himself)*. But it is not so bad. Because in this absolute absence of relevance there is a kind of peace. Maybe it is not joy but simply peace.

So whatever can be known is not true.

And what cannot be known either. Maybe there is no truth.

Even when you say there is no truth this is again truth.

Yes, and this is what I said at the beginning: Even to say "I am not" you have to exist. Even to doubt the Existence you must exist.

You say that God cannot know himself, that he doesn't know himself. This shows the total absurdity of any human discourse on this subject.

Yes, and this is the beauty of it, the absurdity.

It is wonderful because if I could say meaningful things it would be terrible...

It would be absolutely horrible. If somebody could say something meaningful it would be hell. Thanks God, there is no sense you could talk about. I am talking about this irrelevance. About the joy of irrelevance. Nothing can ever grasp what God is.

So I really shouldn't keep seeking.

Oh, keep on, it doesn't matter! Whether you seek or not doesn't make any difference. For God there is no difference. You may see that consciousness, which is already an imagination, will always have the desire to seek what it is. It cannot help you to be what you are nor to rest in that what can never rest. No Spirit can help you. Never.

My grandmother has been my biggest master. The best pointer she gave me was when I was four or five years old. Once I was crying because I had lost my toy, then she told me: "Come here, my boy, sit down, calm down, close your eyes. And now, what do you see?" "Nothing", I said. "So, that belongs to you", she stated. And I can repeat this here now.

For you who was a farmer's son, working on the land was maybe like a Zen practice?

Yes, like anything, being a farmer, milking cows, one never knows. I think that all steps lead to the absence of steps. No way out. In the dream, forgetting what you are will always change in remembering it. But in forgetting as in remembering you are what you are. So you never lost or gained anything. There is always this dreamlike forgetting and this dreamlike remembering, and it is in forgetting and in remembering that you realize yourself. The only quality is that Existence itself is in all there is, no more no less.

Wisdom misleads us, and so does love. Everything - as you believe it - that can bring you That what you are, can only mislead you. May it be the intellect, wisdom or love, whatever you imagine, nothing can bring you That what you are. Never ever. So it is only about entertainment simply because you don't need it. Thus there is no expectation and you can enjoy. Nothing can bring you whatsoever, isn't it wonderful?

Is it total renunciation?

No, it is even renouncing renunciation, renouncing the renouncer by being what you are in spite of the renouncer. Whether he renounces or not, who cares?

I know that I cannot understand or know what I am, yet I keep hoping for it. Is there no way to have a glimpse of That?

There are many ways to indicate it and they always indicate what you are, yet you will never know yourself in the relative. In the Absolute you know yourself without any doubt. It is a knowledge without knower, totally prior to him. It is absolute, never relative. I can only indicate that you can never be what you can know or imagine. It is rather expressed in the negative: be what you cannot not be. And everything you can imagine is only a shadow. So don't be a shadow of yourself, be what is the source of all shadows and has no source in itself.

When Jesus says: "When you make the two one... / then will you enter the Kingdom" what is the meaning of his words?

The answer always refers to eternal Life, which is before the first experience and after the last one. Which comes down to talk about the absolute nakedness, about the absence of the absence of a person. This nakedness is an indication of the Absolute, which knows no second. And without a second, That what is absolute cannot control anything because to control you need two. This is called paradise, where there is no second that can be controlled by a first and therefore no second that can control the first. This is the freedom which knows no freedom, free from a second, free, free...

17

You cannot escape from loving yourself

LOGION 113

His disciples said to him:
- When will the kingdom come?
- It will not come by waiting for it.
It will not be a matter of saying:
'here it is' or 'there it is.'
Rather, the kingdom of the father is spread out upon the earth,
and men do not see it.

The Kingdom is what is prior to the awareness of being, because this first mirror of existence is the presence of the first experience. This awareness is the most subtle form of existence, the purest mirror, but it already belongs to imagination.

Isn't awakening precisely to see that everything is there? And when I say to see, I really mean with the eyes.

This will never be visible: the eye cannot see itself and whatever the eye sees cannot be That what is the eye.

But what we see in some state of consciousness is not any more what we see when we are in the ego.

In the ego there is nothing. The ego itself belongs to imagination. How could an imagination find itself in another imagination? The ego has no power.

"The kingdom of the father is spread out upon the earth / and men do not see it".

The paradise is not to come, it is already there but not as a personal paradise. The paradise is where there is no "mine". Nobody will ever be the owner of it because what is mine refers to the separate ego.

Through the absolute aspect of imagination everything is there, the present like the past and the future.

Yes, there is no time or no-time. Everything is. It is the symbol of the infinite. The loop. It is a perpetual motion upward and downward and it is endless because it never started. But the ego which lives from hope thinks that one day there will be a circumstance where it is possible for him to disappear, and by this very hope the absolute ego becomes relative. It is through the understanding of the infinite that the relative, what is the ego, the "I", disappears.

It is scary to walk in the void.

Jesus talks about this abyss: Fear not what you are because you are the absolute abyss. And to be afraid of what you are is ignorance.

The whole history is precisely in the body, in the survival instinct of the body.

This is the folly of thinking that we are born. So fear is there. Whatever idea of existence brings fear and since any idea lives from imagination, it has to be proved. And in order to do so, it always needs a second imagination. The void is unbearable because the void means absence of duality: in it there is not even this first imagination and without duality no first either, naturally. So to be afraid of That, of what we are, namely of what is without duality, is rather stupid. We cannot imagine how stupid we can be.

It can be cured.

Yes, we can cure stupidity. And whatever we can cure belongs to stupidity because Knowledge doesn't need to be cured, it is unconditional. Stop making efforts and the stupidity will disappear on its own accord, as it came. So "be quiet and see". The stupidity that came will go but That what is knowledge is before, during and after everything that is.

How is it possible that the Absolute takes itself for the relative?

You will never be able to solve this mystery. By falling in love with an idea of yourself, by waking up to this first "I" thought - the first idea of existence - you already are outside. If you take the first appearance of light for truth, for what you are, you go out of what you are and enter imagination. And you cannot do otherwise, you will always fall in love with what you are, again and again. Thus there is you and the object of your love, me and myself, it is unavoidable. But you have to be That what you are in spite of this love story of "me and myself", because you will always fall in love again. You cannot help it and because of this love for yourself you want to know yourself. By knowing himself God falls in ignorance. When God knows God he becomes an object of knowledge and at that very moment he falls in the darkness of ignorance.

An awakened being is finished with this love story.

No, there is no idea of finished, nor of before, nor of after. The beauty is that there never has been and never will be an awakened being just as there never will be a being who is not awakened. Both are ideas.

18
The only suicide you can commit

*

LOGION 24

His disciples said to him:
Show us the place where you are,
since it is necessary for us to seek it.
He said to them:
Whoever has ears, let him hear.
There is light within a man of light,
and he lights up the whole world.
If he does not shine, he is darkness.

For one who wants to know what the world is, what is there to light up? First we have to define at which level we are speaking.

At the level of the Absolute.

So there is nothing to do. No enlightenment! When Ramana Maharshi was asked if he was enlightened, realized, his answer was: "What you see as Ramana can never be realized but That what is the Self is always realized". At the level of the relative there is nobody, so you cannot do anything, and at the level of the Absolute nothing can be done. So what to say? Again, be what you are.

Exactly, what to say about this story of enlightenment?

It's a fairy tale... "truth" is another fairy tale.

I wonder if this logion doesn't mean that we all are enlightened.

It doesn't mean that there is no one who is not enlightened or that there is such a thing as an enlightened one, but only that there never was and never will be some *one* who is or is not enlightened, because all is the Self.

For me, "the light within a man" is not the same thing as an enlightened man. Usually "enlightened" means realized, awakened.

Yes, and I say, all this is not!

Jesus said: "I am the light".

He is the light but he didn't say "I am enlightened". It is totally different.

This logion says: "There is light within a man of light".

Jesus is the light of the light.

"If he does not shine, he is darkness". Can a man be darkness?

Yes, when the Self takes himself for a relative object, there is darkness. It is a suicide: God takes himself for an object and this is the only suicide you can commit.

If God is being misled, if the Self is mistaken, so there, we are doomed...

Of course, who else? Is there anything apart from God? If God is taking himself for an object, he is no more absolute. And not being this Absolute that you are is the only suicide you can commit.

There is only one Self, how can It take Itself for...?

There is not such thing as "only one Self", there is *only* the Self. No, the Self is not one, otherwise It would be called unity. But it is called non-duality. The fact that there is no second doesn't mean that there is "one". The Self is all there is. And there is no such thing as "one" because one always needs two. One is already darkness, ignorance. Even the *idea* of Self is ignorance. To be the Self is not to know it, neither one nor two, a total absence of what you are or what you are not.

I think that the disciples' question, "Show us the place where you are", is stupid and has irritated Jesus, who then answered: "Whoever has ears, let him hear!".

This would be an interpretation. Actually the answer depends on the questioner. When Ramana Maharshi was asked "Where will you go and where can we look for you?", he gave a similar answer: "You say I am going away, but where can I go? I am always here".

This is exactly what Jesus said in logion 77:

It is I who am the light which is above them all.
It is I who am the all.
From me did the all come forth,
and unto me did the all extend.
Split a piece of wood, and I am there.
Lift up the stone, and you will find me there.

And the beginning of logion 50 is totally in accordance with this logion 24:

Jesus said:
If they say to you:
Where did you come from?
say to them:
We came from the light,
the place where the light came into being
on its own accord...

Yes, you are That from where the light came. That indicates the Absolute source. And the first presence of Existence is the light.

From this light came the Spirit and the form, because light is the source of everything that is. Thus light is all there is but you, you are the source of it.

So every being is luminous.

No, not human beings, not the man, That what *is* the man! You are pure light... there is only light, which is the essence of all there is. Your nature is the source of this light. So light is the first presence of your existence but you are even prior to that. Thus be yourself a light, take the light as the absolute mirror of your absolute existence. From this mirror arises an infinite realization. You are the source of this light and you are the source of all that arises.

Since you are the Absolute dreamer, you can say that you are even the Absolute dream, you cannot divide. And in this Absolute dream there are stones that you can lift. And you are the stone, and you are the lifting, and you are the space. There is nothing but That what you are, as the dreamer and as the dream, no difference. There is space, but there is no space. There is a stone, but there is no stone. It is always a paradox and you are this paradox. When there is a form, you are That what is this form. When there is the formless Spirit, you are That what is this formless Spirit. And when there is awareness, you are this awareness. You are always what is, because there is nothing but what you are.

We think that there are comings and goings whilst nothing happens. What to do? For me, the main thing is always to indicate the quality of Existence. Nothing can be gained through understandings, and through misunderstandings nothing can be lost. This is the quality of Knowledge itself, or of God. In forgetting, God cannot forget himself, and in remembering, there is nothing he can remember. There is always forgetting and remembering but none of them can be an advantage or a disadvantage. This is the nature of this Existence you are.

Movement and repose.

Movement or non-movement, both are concepts which cannot

bring anything. Nothing can be removed from what you are or added to it. Nothing can be given from anything. This is the quality of everyone's nature, namely of this Life that you are. Therefore all this understanding has no value, thanks God. There is nothing in understanding, and this is joy. Just as you never lost anything in ignorance, there is nothing to gain in understanding. It is merely an entertainment, it is the joy of Existence. Understanding may occur but nothing can be gained by it. Thus there is no necessity for an understanding to be there or not there.

Otherwise you fall back into causality and it is no longer the Absolute. I am without a cause.

I would simply stay quiet without saying that "I am this or that". Even the Absolute becomes a concept.

Where does this conviction come from that is in all of us that we are That which is unknowable, ungraspable, unverifiable? Doesn't it seem absurd?

As I said, in your love story you will always try to know yourself. There is no escape. You will always try to find a better fitting word, like "absolute" or "more absolute", blah-blah ... This is Self-entertainment. And this entertainment is the realization of what you are: without cause or reason, it simply is.

A dream object asks why there is a dream seeking. And it will always be so. It is a dream questioner, a dream answerer, a dream question, like: "Oh, why are there six billion and a half ignorant people, why are so few interested in truth?". With the idea of "one" you create six billion and a half human beings.

There are no human beings, not even one, so where is the problem? But if there is only one human being, with him you create the whole universe, and this becomes your reality. Bur this is a dream, what to do? In this dream there are numerous solutions, but they only are dream solutions. They cannot help you to find out what you are. In the dream there is one who says: "I am the Absolute". Do you think God cares about him? Whether you say

"I am a stone" or "I am the Absolute" it makes no difference, both are a dream.

The advice often given by gurus to their disciples, "Know yourself", is it also a dream solution? If I understood well we cannot know ourselves.

Ramana Maharshi indicates how: know yourself as you know yourself in deep sleep. You exist in the total absence of somebody who knows or doesn't know. And this existence is Knowledge itself, totally unconditioned, without any necessity, void of whatever individual. Knowing or not knowing, world or no world, you are what is. And this is Knowledge itself. This, you know it by Heart and not by understanding, by wisdom, by love or by whatever you can imagine. You know That before imagining. This is Knowledge.

The word "knowledge" seems inappropriate because you refer to this knowledge that I have in deep sleep...

No, you don't *have* any knowledge: it is not a matter of having or possessing. It is the knowledge that you exist, which is in spite of all your ideas of existence. This simply indicates the Knowledge which is in spite of all relative knowledge, of all knower or non-knower. Otherwise it becomes a word. When you try to know, you are trying to bring That into this relative world. You can never put Knowledge into a relative, objective knowledge.

This is why it is always indicated in a negative way by "neti-neti". By subtracting all that can be subtracted you become only the substratum, God, the Self. Whatever idea arises, it is not that. It is neither knowledge nor non-knowledge. That is what master Eckhart was calling "the groundless ground", the very ground of knowledge. God who doesn't even know God, the Self which doesn't know the Self, is what we call Knowledge. Nothing of what you say can be the Tao. But still we can talk about it, why not? The Tao is a big book like that, simply to say that you cannot be something we can talk about.

If pages are continuously erased, are we merely writing on them for fun?

There is no page which can be erased or created. There, all pages are infinite. Nothing has ever been created, nothing will ever be destroyed. There is neither Creation nor destruction. The next moment is already there, absolute in itself. No coming and going.

In order to be this experiencer who experiences whatever can be experienced, you have to forget your Absolute nature. Somehow, you have to do as if you were a person, so you play with this idea but maybe you forget that it is only a play. It is as if you were in a doll house, as if you were playing with dolls for some time and had forgotten that you are not a doll. By taking yourself for a relative object in time, you became a simple marionette. And I am here to remind you: "Hey, what are you doing? Are you playing or what?"

Be in the world but not of the world, that's all. Know yourself by being That what is prior. You are always in this game, which cannot give you anything or take anything from you. It is not about going out of the game or of whatever. Know yourself by That what has nothing to gain or lose in this world, because you never lost anything there and will never gain anything either. The truth is, you cannot leave what you are: this is what you are and you will never go out of it. No way out. Never mind whether you have the tunnel vision of a person or the open vision of consciousness, you are what you are in any circumstance. You are That what never needs a change to be what it is, and this only is the quality of the Existence you are. And every time you need to know something to become what you are, it may be a pleasant game but without any value, thanks God!

19
A totality of Being, which is never born and never dies

๛

LOGION 32

Jesus said:
A city being built on a high mountain
and fortified
cannot fall,
nor can it be hidden.

When the Spirit turns to That what is the origin of the Spirit the world is no more a danger. That is more than solid. That can never be destroyed or endangered. When awareness turns to itself, it is as if an imperturbable silence descends. Therefore That is called "the highest", which can never be lost. Everything else can be endangered, all possessions, all that you can know, but when the light turns to itself there is this unshakable silence, which can never be covered or uncovered.

So this silence is out of time.

Time? Beautiful idea! Yes, time is also the idea of duality, the idea of existence, namely the original folly, which is to believe that something exists in something else. The truth is, it is a story, an infinite story already belonging to consciousness, which is the root of time.

"In the beginning was the Word, and the Word was with God, and the Word was God". This is the Prologue of the Gospel of John.

Yes, the Word is the father, the idea of Father. It is awareness, the source. It is not different from God, yet it is not God, it is That what is God. From the Word comes the root thought "I", the first light, then "I am", the absolute Spirit, then "I am so and so", the matter. Awareness is the first manifestation of Being, the first presence which makes it possible to feel existence. It is the Word, the first sound, Om, the subtlest "I".

"The Word became flesh and made his dwelling among us", John continues. Is there a will at the origin of this?

No, because this never happened. There was no beginning. The idea of a beginning belongs to time. That what is God has no beginning or end. And the manifestation either. That *is* God, potential or manifested: there is only what is God.

There is the idea of time, the idea of a beginning, the idea that something happened, the idea that God woke up. But God never woke up. He is awakening, he is awareness and unawareness in themselves. And there is no beginning, neither here, nor in the world, and you are That, now and for ever!

Can we say that the illusion of relativity is sui generis, born from itself?

No, it didn't appear, That is always present, the Absolute of Being. The illusion already belongs to illusion. There is no illusion, there nothing but God. Only an illusion can speak of illusion. For God there is none. God doesn't know himself and God doesn't know any illusion. Only when God knows himself is there truth and illusion: we need "two" to say that something is an illusion.

But for That, there is neither truth nor illusion. For God, no veil needs to fall because for him there never was any veil. There is nothing that can or must exist. Thousands of veils can fall, and nothing happens. So there is no gain possible for what you are or for what is God.

What is fatal in the idea that a veil can be lifted is the hope that one day it *will* be lifted, and this expectation can only exist in time. If the vision of the illusion were real, it would be possible to realize in time That what doesn't know time. And it would be hell! The hope of seeing a veil being lifted projects you in time, so you find yourself in the folly of making God a relative object, which sees himself in the necessity of a change. If a veil were to be lifted or a light were to appear or whatever idea, this would make God a conditioned being. And wanting to change what you are in something else is pure folly, because in this way you create an image of yourself and think that it is you. And this is duality.

"There is a very fine line between paranoia and metanoia",
Émile Gillabert said.

Yes, there is nothing between the two. Sanity and insanity come together. They are both sides of the coin.

We can say that all of this is Existence.

We can, but we don't have to. We can do many things but we don't have to do them. We can define, we can make an image, and it doesn't change anything. This is the unconditioned Being, in whatever condition, yes or no, for or against, hither and thither, none of this affects That what you are, and this is joy: no gain, no loss, in whatever circumstances. Nothing ever began and nothing will ever stop the realization of what you are. You will be raped by yourself, again and again, this is the dead end of your existence and you cannot escape from it. Whether you are raped or loved by yourself, who cares? That what is freedom is always free, it is the absence of a second which could rape. But there will always be the imagination of a struggle against oneself... continuously. In this world, through all kind of struggles, consciousness will always care about its so-called truth.

Could we say that it is absolute nihilism? The nothing of Nothing?

Yes, in the sense that nothing happens. Nothing is born, nothing dies. It is Eternal Life, which never appears or disappears. There is no coming and going, neither in awareness, nor in the consciousness "I am", nor in the world. This moment is as absolute as what it is made of: it is a totality of Being which is never born and never dies.

❧

20
You will never be able to detach yourself from what you are

❧

LOGION 13

Jesus said to his disciples:
Compare me to someone and tell me whom I am like.
Simon Peter said to him:
You are like a righteous angel.
Matthew said to him:
You are like a wise philosopher.
Thomas said to him:
Master, my mouth is wholly incapable of saying
whom you are like.
Jesus said:
I am not your master.
Because you have drunk,
you have become intoxicated from the bubbling spring
which I have measured out.
And he took him and withdrew and told him three things.
When Thomas returned to his companions, they asked him:
What did Jesus say to you?
Thomas said to them:

If I tell you one of the things which he told me,
you will pick up stones and throw them at me;
a fire will come out of the stones
and burn you up.

I very much appreciate the moments when we don't speak.

Anyway, during all that time, nobody said anything. I talked you to death so that silence comes. Buddha said: I preached for forty years and I never said a single word to any one. This was his whole teaching. This is an absolute indication of the irrelevance of words, the joy of a speech which leads nowhere.

Concerning Buddha, the success of the non-teaching is total: he taught so little that, as soon as he died, his disciples made a legend of his birth: his mother gave birth standing, holding onto the branch of a tree and, the moment he was born, he stood up.

Yes, the disciples are the founders of the religions, then the world takes over by creating a martyr or a mystic so that there is no danger, otherwise the Teaching cannot remain in this world. So its height is immediately raised where there is no danger.

Jesus himself was said to be begotten by Immaculate Conception. It is totally crazy!

This has nothing to do with the body, but indicates that the nature of Jesus is unborn and consequently cannot be conceived by a body. Nisargadatta said the same: What I am never came out of a vagina. For what I am, there is neither a mother nor a son. It simply means that no person was ever born and in reality, there is no such thing as a mother or a son.

Thus the Immaculate Conception indicates that what is Jesus is unborn. There was no conception, in whatever way. Buddhists depict this in a similar way: on a parchment, one can first see two naked bodies having sex, and then a baby being born of one of them. And by tilting the parchment, one can see two skeletons conceiving a third one: the dead give birth to the dead. Life is without birth. Jesus was never born of a person, like here, nobody is born of a body.

Why do millions of men settle for such unlikely stories?

Because the little phantom always needs to have some importance. He needs a family, an origin, a goal, because without stories he would not exist. He would have no weight. Thus there is the mother, the story of the family, the story of humanity, and all of this comes from the first existential crisis.

I like this sentence from "Corpus Hermeticum": "Only the same knows the same". I think there is no way to make it shorter.

Only the Self knows the Self by being the Self and not by comparing. Thus Jesus is the Redeemer who frees you from the idea of redemption, because you will never be able to detach yourself from what you are, impossible! There is no redemption for what you are. Redemption would mean that something should detach itself from something else. But there is no first or second from which That could detach itself, because you are what *is*. That will never be able to detach Itself from Itself.

But in logion 108, Jesus does speak of a revelation, of a lifting of a veil.

Jesus said:
He who will drink from my mouth
will become like me.
I myself shall become he,
and the things that are hidden
will be revealed to him.

Yes, it is a vision but it is not what the redemption is. For me, the crucifixion shows that the redemption is impossible and there is no way out. The main point is the despair, because any hope of redemption implies that you are somebody who needs to be saved.

The impossibility of redemption is the redemption of the idea of redemption, so that even this idea "I" disappears, because in this despair nobody can remain.

In logion 83 we see clearly the functioning of a veil hiding the light, which explains the reason of all those beliefs.

> *Jesus said:*
> *The images are manifest to man,*
> *but the light in them remains concealed*
> *in the image of the light of the father.*
> *He will become manifest,*
> *but his image will remain concealed by his light.*

Even enlightenment is an image hiding enlightenment, just as the image of freedom hides freedom. And if the redemption is an idea, it hides the Absolute. Any idea hides that what is truth, never mind which idol it creates. To make an image already means in itself that it hides.

If you keep saying "no" to anything we say, if you keep pulling more rugs out from under our feet, it becomes more and more crazy! You are right, we have to keep quiet.

No, no, no! Again an image, again an attempt to control by trying to create a necessity for Existence, as if Existence were only in silence. It is pure arrogance. Whether we speak or remain silent, nothing speaks through the words, and nothing keeps quiet in the silence. They are different circumstances that are devoid of meaning.

Silence is permanent and the beauty is that nothing can interrupt it. It is never hidden, so it can never be revealed, because it is not something which can be hidden, or which can keep quiet, or of which we can speak endlessly. Otherwise we could think that we can control it by keeping quiet. For me, arrogance is the idea that we can control That what is Existence by the way we behave. Don't be anything in particular because arrogance means to be something in particular, and this is madness since it places you outside of Existence, that is why!

This creates the wars of religion.

It is always the case when we fight for truth: first we make an image of truth, then we fight for this image, and this is the world. This shows again that consciousness fights continuously for truth without ever reaching it. Since it must keep on fighting at all costs, it endlessly creates religions and images, which follow from this Self-inquiry. It will never stop because it never had a beginning. I am happy that, in all this diversity, *what is* doesn't change. For me, this is actually the miracle. There are so many different concepts, so many ways of seeing, perspectives are countless, and yet nothing changes.

There are not two waves which are the same.

Everything is unique. Among all religions, among all concepts, if a single element were to disappear, there would be no more Existence because everything is exactly as it should be. So does it change anything to have faith or not? Whether one keeps quiet or speaks, nothing changes. And yet it is always different. Wonderful!

The Source in its abundance is constantly overflowing with a superfluous excess of water. And this, I am! Totally superfluous, useless, totally irrelevant, it is a total waste. But in spite of all this overflow, the Source doesn't lose anything of what it is: they are endless and inexhaustible images.

I can only point that the nature of Existence is Silence, and silence is never forced by what is, no matter the way it manifests itself. Circumstances can never condition what is their source. To be That is the quality of Existence, and the rest fluctuates constantly. No matter how high the faiths, the religions or the opinions are, they will never reach That what is Existence in itself. The beauty is that it is always in *spite* of everything which is. Never because.

For me, logion 13 is one of the logia where Jesus manifested himself to the fullest by saying nothing. I find it fantastic that he doesn't say a word!

To remain in the un-said, the only answer is silence.

Actually, to explain to people that they are indefinable is quite a shock!

It is the deadliest shock! It kills instantly.

This is why Thomas cannot say anything to the apostles, otherwise they would throw stones at him.

They would kill him! The initiation of the Heart is this Silence that you cannot name or describe, it is not the space, the Spirit. Silence is a mortal shock which breaks your heart. It breaks an imaginary heart so that only the Heart remains, the Heart which doesn't know the Heart. So space is still a false heart. First it starts with the body, then comes the space or the Spirit, then awareness. But the first and last experience, which is the light, is already false. That what is silence is prior to the light. And That breaks all ideas!

This is taking us to the abyss.

There is no abyss. For the "me", the worst thing is to see that nobody needs to jump. And nobody asks you to do so: you are so irrelevant that there is no necessity. The biggest jump is to see that there is nobody who needs to jump!

We cannot even commit suicide!

You cannot kill what IS and who needs that the phantom is killed? Only a phantom needs analogies, initiation, etc. The real initiation of the Heart is that the Heart never needs to be initiated, never needs to be more open either. This has nothing to do with love. This *is* love! And even to say this is still too much.

Only a relative God has a heart. The Heart never owns anything. Ownership begins with the owner owning what can be owned. And all of this is a relationship, a love affair: a lover loves, and through this love he creates the beloved.

But at some point he starts to hate that he loves: then he becomes a seeker. He wants to return home, but there is no way home. No direction home! Whatever he does confirms that he needs something, but there is no solution. This indicates that there is no way out, never ever! This is Absolute nakedness, and this is Jesus.

21
The split second which splits the second

✤

LOGION 2

Jesus said:
Let him who seeks
continue seeking until he finds.
When he finds,
he will become troubled.
When he becomes troubled,
he will be astonished,
and he will rule over the All.

W*hy do we have this desire to seek?*

Because you are in love with yourself, and love makes you blind to what you are. Love makes you different from what you are: you are a lover, therefore different from your beloved. This is the very seed of desire. Thus you desire your beloved, you desire yourself, because you fall in love with yourself. And being different from what you are makes you suffer. Only what you call love can make you so crazy about yourself! This is the biggest trap there is, and you cannot avoid it. And not wanting to love yourself only comes from loving yourself. Fantastic!

So it seems that the Absolute realizes itself in the love of itself. It becomes the lover, the loving and the beloved. It is the way It realizes itself. And the lover will always want to know the beloved. No way out. Always nostalgic for itself, the lover cannot stop meditating on its nature, whatever the experience may be. The very nature of the realization is this desire of the lover for his beloved. Love is the highest that the lover can reach in his attempt to know the beloved, but he will never succeed to know him. Thus the Self will never know the Self, and the desire will never end. No hope. The tragicomedy of Romeo and Juliet is that both have to die. But for whom?

You can say that the realization happens like this: the realizer tries to realize the realizer, but he never succeeds, and this is the way Reality realizes itself. It is an endless story because there will always be the next moment, and the next, and the next. And every moment is the absolute Existence meditating on itself. Thus you must be what you are in spite of all of this and not because you find or you know yourself. You are in spite of this love story, whether it is there or not. And That, there is no way you cannot become it. Therefore That what you are cannot be reached and never needs to be reached because you *are* That.

Can the seeking for the experiencer eradicate him?

No. When you seek for him, he is gone. You cannot eradicate something which never was there. This is why this takes us to the direct path: seek for the seer, and you cannot find him. There never was anybody who perceived or experienced.

Ask the question "Who am I?", then remain as "I am", because this unpronounced "I am" is the answer to the question "Who am I?". From the pronounced, you go to what is unpronounced:

then you are prior to the pronouncer. In this question, "who" falls first, then the void, the Spirit, then the "I" which you experience as awareness. And you are the absolute answer to the absolute question "Who am I?".

It is a good method...

If the method is supposed to work, it will work, otherwise you can practice it for millions of years and it will make no difference. You will never know how it will happen: you can realize yourself with the question "Who am I?" or with putting butter on a slice of bread, and you will never know when. But anyway, it will happen!

Then, surprise! You are surprised by what you are. An Absolute surprise: you are the treasure you were looking for! You were trying to find this treasure which had never been hidden. You wanted to understand the Knowledge which was always there. What an astonishment!

Can the method of neti-neti, which consists of saying "not this, not that", takes us somewhere?

Yes, it takes you to "I am".

No more? Isn't it possible to remove "I am" with neti-neti?

No, this is why we speak of Grace. At the beginning a master may be there to reach "I am", but after, it is the end of this relationship, because in "I am" there is no master and no disciple. And no neti-neti either. There is the void that you cannot reduce. It is always possible to change states, you can have the experience to be the void, but even the void is not what you are.

What to think of Grace?

Grace is your nature, the nature of the Self, the nature of God. Grace is not to know Grace. Grace is the Self which doesn't know the Self. Grace is to be the Kingdom. And the Kingdom has no king. By being Grace, there is only Grace. But Grace is pitiless. Pity comes from a pitiful God who pities himself, then others. Compassion, the nature of Grace, never shows mercy. It drops you as if it never knew you, every night: it is totally devoid of mercy. And if you run after it, it is nowhere to be found.

But we cannot run after Grace.

If you look for Grace, you cannot find it anywhere. Grace will find you, it is already after you. And when it is after you, there is no way out. It is everywhere. No place without it. You are sentenced to happiness. Pitiless, merciless...

So this neti-neti takes you to the void, but still this is not what you are. By not finding yourself in the void through neti-neti, there is like a resignation. You give up the words, then you give up the void, because you see that even there you cannot find who you are.

Then there is silence. It breaks your heart not to be able to find yourself in any circumstance. Everything started because you wanted to know your beloved. Seeing that you cannot find him, the love story with yourself collapses, and your heart is broken. This is called the split second which splits the second, the idea of a heart, the idea of a lover. No more lover or beloved. And this broken heart is what you are.

Then, surprise, there is peace: what you wanted is already there and always was there. It is That what is never never, That in which the whole drama of this love story appears. It is and always will be in spite of everything. In spite of forgetting in the dream where you fell in love, and in spite of remembering in the dream where love dropped by itself, you are what you are. It is nothing new, That was always there as Silence and not as something you could have experienced. All the deep understandings or visions that you can count have no value, thanks God, because without the infinite presence of what you are, there could be no forgetting or remembering. So be what you cannot not be.

22
It is an absolute non-knowledge

❦

LOGION 44

Jesus said:
Whoever blasphemes against the father
will be forgiven,
and whoever blasphemes against the son
will be forgiven,
but whoever blasphemes against the holy spirit
will not be forgiven either on earth or in heaven.

D oesn't this logion describe a form of suicide of this Eternal which is in us? Isn't the Kingdom of God the place of the Spirit, the supreme freedom ?

This is reminiscent of the temptation of Christ in what has been called the desert. The devil offered to make him the king, the emperor of the universe [1]. But Jesus is not tempted by this power because he says, "My Kingdom is not of this world[2]". Nevertheless it is certain that the dualist idea "me and myself", or the kingdom of this world, the universe, always remains a temptation, the temptation of what you can call the devil. Wanting to know yourself is always a temptation of control, but everything you know makes you dependent because the knower depends on what he knows, so it is always a dependent knowledge.

(1) "All this I will give you, if you will bow down and worship me." (Matt. 4:9). "I will give you all this power and glory. It has been handed over to me, and I can give it to whomever I choose." (Luke 4:6).

(2) "Away from me, Satan! For it is written: 'Worship the Lord your God, and serve him only." (Matthew 4:10; Deuteronomy 6:13). "Jesus, knowing that they intended to come and make him king by force, withdrew again to a mountain by himself." (John 6:15).

The supreme freedom is when freedom doesn't know freedom, because the freedom you can know can only be a prison. The freedom of the Absolute, or of this Supreme, is to be free from a second and be what is. But the freedom of a person is different: it is a dependent freedom. And to give up the freedom that you are for the freedom of the universe, yes, it is what we can call a suicide. So if you give up the freedom that you are for the knowledge of what you are, the knowledge of this Supreme or any knowledge of the world, any treasure you can gain, you lose the Kingdom of what you are, the paradise.

Again, to be this nakedness you must give up all that is "mine", in this way you gain the knowledge of this absolute Kingdom that you are. You cannot take anything with you because an owner will never go to this paradise [1]. It is like going through awareness or through the light, because the light is a door which doesn't let any idea in. If you come as you are, without any luggage, not even "one who is without luggage", then you are welcome. This is why Ramana Maharshi spoke of renouncing renunciation, renouncing the renouncer.

(2) "It is easier for a camel to go through the eye of a needle than for someone who is rich to enter the kingdom of God" (Mark 10:25, Luke 18:25, Matthew 19:24).

One who doesn't praise himself deprives himself of Life, he "blasphemes against the Holy Spirit".

I would call that the only suicide you can commit: not to be what you are. Every time you are not what you are it is a suicide. This is the true meaning of suicide, and not killing the body or whatever. To be an imagination, an object in time, is a suicide but, thanks God, this cannot be killed because it never existed. So no harm: an infinite suicide, and nothing happens. But again, every time you are not what you are, you can say it is a suicide.

But even at that moment, I am always what I am…

… the mind says, so that it can remain as "me". This is the devil speaking.

How could I not be what I am?

"Even ignorant, I am what I am", the devil says, who wants to stay ignorant. Again a trick of the mind!

I don't understand.

Yes, I know. Surely the mind doesn't understand, because if there were understanding, there would be no more mind. This is the devil avoiding at all costs to understand that there is nothing to understand, because when you say "But I am anyway what I am", you speak from an understanding, so that you can stay ignorant. As I just said, every moment of this ignorance is a suicide. This may be the meaning of blaspheming against the Spirit: you enter this hell of separation.

This means that I take this separation for real.

No, there again, there is "my" understanding: "I am anyway what I am, I have understood". But this understanding needs somebody, and this is what you are defending. Whatever you understood, you have to defend it as you just did. It is tricky, totally tricky! This is why the devil is called Lucifer: he wants to bring light where there is already light. The master of knowledge!

The world is there only because there is the devil, but for That what is God, there is neither devil nor world. When there is God there is only God, and God doesn't know God. But when God knows himself he becomes the devil. And with this knowledge, he creates the world.

"My kingdom is not of this world", Jesus says.

(1) John 18:36.

Yes, those words refer to That what is prior to the devil and to the world, prior to "me and the world", prior to the first enemy "me". And the only enemy I have is "me", the devil. Whatever knowledge, whatever understanding that you have to defend makes you a warlord. This is why the absolute non-knowledge corresponds more with your nature, which never needs to defend itself. You cannot gain or lose your nature. However, even the deepest understanding, you have to defend, and it makes you a soldier. This owner who speaks of "my understanding" can only be the devil, born of "two". This may be the meaning of blaspheming against the Spirit.

If we are all, we are also the darkest.

You are the darkness and you are the light, like in the symbol of the Tao, the black-and-white disk of the Yin and Yang. Light shows itself in light and darkness. So the essence of darkness is the light, because light is all there is, but it is not a light that you can experience.

But regarding logion 24, didn't you say that every being lights up?

> *...There is light within a man of light,*
> *and he lights up the whole world.*
> *If he does not shine,*
> *he is darkness.*

No, I didn't say that every being lights up, I said: it is the light. Light is all there is. You can also say "awareness" instead of "light". But the point is that there is no being who lights up. You can say that a being is an information of light, but what you call a "being" doesn't exist. A being is light, but there is no such thing as light in a being.

We can judge that there is a pedagogical aspect in some logia. The formulation of those words is not absolute. In the first logion, Jesus indeed said that there was an interpretation to be found: "Whoever finds the interpretation of these sayings will not experience death.".

I would take those words as pointers. Even the Gospel of Thomas is not the truth. Same about the Tao. See for yourself.

Picasso said: "I don't search, I find".

He found a lot but he only copied himself. And what harm does it do? The words I am uttering have already been uttered infinite times, yet you cannot say that I stole them from somebody. Even if they are repeated again and again, they always come from the same source, ever fresh, ever new.

It is the same with the artist, but his crime is to think that he can create something: "It is I who did it". There is the suicide: "I am the doer, it belongs to me". Nothing is mine! The artist's arrogance is the devil's arrogance who goes out of "what is" to grab the idea that he creates personally. At that point God leaves his nature and falls in the hell of separation. So there again, we may speak of blaspheming against the Spirit.

When we get together, sometimes there are moments when every one sees the Absolute in the other's body.

It is a recognition. If you want to find an "other" and really search for it, you are surprised to find yourself. In everything that you investigate in order to find its essence, you discover that the essence is what you are. If you investigate this world to find its source, you discover that you are it. There is no way out. All that exists is what you are, no matter which direction you take, wherever you go, you cannot miss yourself!

❧

23
Everything is a fairy tale

❧

Jesus said:
The foxes have their holes
and the birds have their nests,
but the son of man has no place
to lay his head and rest.

There is nowhere you can rest. Otherwise you would create a place, but for what you are there is no home, not a single concept or place, not a single idea or imagination where you can find some rest. By seeing that there will never be any rest, strangely, there is a total rest. You cannot explain this paradox.

Your nature is the absence of rest. You are the infinite wanderer who endlessly goes through different possibilities without this making you different in any way. You endlessly wander in perpetual wonder.

"Become passers-by", logion 42 says.

Like in a waiting room: "Good morning!", then, "Good bye!". You are in a waiting room where the entrance and exit doors are open. You are immovable, you are Silence. You come, "Good morning!" and you go, "Good bye!" and nothing happens.

Be in the world but not of the world. Simply see that what happens in the world cannot bring you anything or take anything from you. This can neither increase nor diminish the quality of what you are. Nothing of what you are can be taken or given. There is the absence of possession, the nakedness of Existence which is the quality in itself but doesn't know any. It is the pointer given in the Bible: "It is easier for a camel to go through the eye of a needle than for a rich man to enter the kingdom of God" [1].

(1) Matthew 19:24; Mark 10:25; Luke 18:25.

When Jesus utters these last words on the cross, "it is finished", does it means that all is dead, all is finished, all is realized?

In the experience of death there is the experience of Life. Such has been Ramana Maharshi's death experience: everything dies but you remain as That what is the Living.

And when Jesus says, "My God, My God, why have You forsaken Me?"?

This could mean: even you, God, have abandoned me. But for me, it is rather the moment when the last hope, the last illusion, disappears, the symbol that What is life doesn't need to be saved. This is not self-pity but probably an expression of joy.

Is this total renunciation?

The recognition that what we are doesn't need the mind.

The mind, which consists of all the thoughts, concepts and images, is the very antithesis of the pure Spirit.

...which is already a concept! Whether you say pure Spirit, consciousness or world, they are concepts. Only the Heart is That. Even the idea of purity is a concept. This very idea is stained.

Intuition is not a concept.

Yes, this too. Whatever can be named pertains to the mind, therefore it is a concept.

Only silence is not a concept.

Even silence is a concept. It is a block of Existence which never appears, never disappears, never has been created. Every moment is infinite in its nature, without beginning or end, and this moment is the way Reality realizes itself. No beginning, no end, no motive, not the slightest need of explanations. All of this is a bunch of stupidities.

Man has always this tendency to create God in his own image.

In order to save himself, man constantly creates an ideal for himself, a golden calf. But whatever we say about God cannot truly define him. Yet, in order to say it, before and after the speaker, That what is the speaker must be. For somebody to exist, somebody who can doubt what he is or not, before the doubting God, there is That what is God. It is the basis of Ramakrishna's teaching: in order to doubt your existence, first you must exist.

After all, everything is a fairy tale. Knowing doesn't mean identity, but for a knower to be, Knowledge must exist before and after him. Knowledge is never conditioned by whatever presence or absence; with or without concepts, you are.

In fact, our different questions demonstrate the multiple variations of the mind.

There are six and a half billion different opinions about the current world situation, and all are right. All are the Absolute points of views of Being itself.

One of your books has a title "The Myth of Enlightenment"...

I only indicated by this that the search will never stop because the spirit is continuously looking for what it is without ever finding it. This never stops. Where the spirit is, there is a search!

We should keep quiet.

What a boring party this would be! No, we can speak, and speak, and speak, and nothing happens. Wonderful! Silence is uninterrupted and nothing can disturb it. The silence which can be disturbed and requires quietness doesn't need to be taken into account. The moment God knows himself as the first, the lover wakes up. And the moment God knows himself as a lover, he leaves his Absolute nature and is already missing what he is. And the search begins...

We cannot find any rest, no place to rest our heads. This is the joy of the absence of a home, the joy of the absence of the absence of a home, the joy of the absence of one who has no home.

As Jesus says to us in this logion, we only have an apparent relationship with the world because nothing of this world concerns us.

Yes, "My Kingdom is not of this world", Jesus says. Light is without experience, without form. It is what is also called the black light or the black sun. Without necessity, without need, without hunger or thirst. Complete satisfaction. Total peace.

The absence of rest is your nature but being born stupid and dying stupid is your condition. You come stupid, you go stupid, and in between you think you know something, which is even more stupid. It starts stupid with Atma, becomes more stupid with "I am", and even more stupid with this body. So, stupid, more stupid and even more stupid... stupidity all the way! Where stupidity begins, Knowledge stops. And where stupidity stops, Knowledge starts. Whatever has a beginning is stupid and whatever finishes is also stupid. Your last cloth is a shroud and this last shirt has no pockets.

We are born naked, we die naked, and in between there is the carnival of Existence. Like a magnet, we are drawing to us everything that attracts us. It is the magnetic power of love, which wants to possess. Then we are afraid to lose what we own. And questions are rising: what is there after death? Will I have the same beautiful car in my next life? Will I be able to take my Mercedes or will I have to start again with a Renault or a Citroen? We always come back to this: any hope is hell.

The end is terrible because it has no beginning. And when it comes, it breaks your heart because at the end, death takes you away and there is no winner.

❧

24
The unshakeable Silence

LOGION 33

Jesus said:
Preach from your housetops
that which you will hear in your ear.
For no one lights a lamp
and puts it under a bushel,
nor does he put it in a hidden place,
but rather he sets it on a lampstand
so that everyone who enters and leaves
will see its light.

Have this experience of being a light unto yourself, be That what is light, be what you are, light itself, and be a light in the world. From the silence you are, express the silence. From the unpronounced silence, pronounce the silence. This doesn't belong to you: it is like speaking to yourself, and this is the meaning of this logion.

But talking to oneself is a monologue.

It is always a monologue, from "I" to "I", without claiming anything. It is being the Absolute owner, Existence itself. To be what is, then to expound the presence of this existence.

Doesn't this go against logion 93, which says:

Do not give what is holy to dogs,
lest they throw them on the dung-heap.
Do not throw the pearls to swine,
lest they turn them into mud.

It is not the opposite. When you talk to yourself there are no more swine. But if you are a teacher and pretend to know, you are claiming something, it is as if you had a pearl which you exhibit to others. And if you talk to somebody else, it is indeed like throwing pearls to swine.

When you say "talking to ourselves", does it mean that at one point we realize that even the world is ourselves and there is no difference?

Nobody realizes this. By being That which is prior and beyond, you are the origin of the first, the second and the third states. By being the Heart you *are* Reality, but there is no   who realizes. Little difference... It is Silence. The realization doesn't create a realized person.

So, all of those who claim they are awakened...

... Are still asleep.

If I say that I have realized...

It is totally non-realized! It is ignorance.

Logion 34 says practically the same:

Jesus said:
If a blind man leads a blind man,
they will both fall into a pit.

Yes, if a blind man leads a blind man, both end up in the darkness of ignorance and not in the darkness of light. It makes a little difference... In the darkness of ignorance there is somebody who is in darkness, but in the darkness of light there is the absolute absence of the presence of a person. Then darkness is not darkness. Again, the nudity of the Heart is the absence of ownership. It is the kingdom of consciousness, a kingdom without a king. You cannot experience yourself, you can only be it. The absolute Seer can never be seen, and the relative seer already belongs to the scenery.

One thing strikes me in this logion: at the beginning Jesus uses the image of sound, and then the image of light. But light is Silence. And when we go from words to silence, words take us to silence.

No, no, you don't go from words to silence. Silence speaks and Silence keeps quiet. The silence is not different. But talking about somebody who speaks and somebody who listens is different from the Silence. Speaking, listening and keeping quiet are the Silence by nature, but somebody who is quiet, a group who doesn't talk, is not the Silence. Somebody who doesn't say anything is still too noisy! There is still somebody pretending to be quiet.

Karl, you never leave us the possibility to say "I", no way to hide!

No way to claim anything. Existence cannot be owned: you can only be it. You are Silence, but it will never be your silence. I am here to prevent you from hiding behind an intellectual understanding. All the carpets will be removed, no comfort, no understanding to comfort you. All of this is ignorance.

This logion ends with those words, "so that everyone who enters and leaves will see its light". Furthermore, you have mentioned the light of Shiva. What is the light of Shiva?

The light of Shiva is awareness.

But aware of itself?

No, the light is the highest experience of Existence, but even this experience is not Shiva, it is the purest reflection of Shiva but not That what is Shiva.

So the light is already too late.

No, it is not too late, it is simply the beginning and the end of the realization. Reality is prior and beyond but the realization begins with the light and ends with the light.

And love, is it still prior?

The lover begins and ends with the light. Prior to the light, prior to the lover, there is That what is the lover, That what is Brahman, the Self, God, the absolute non-knowledge, which is not even experiencing to be, neither being nor non-being, the Mystery itself. Light is the beginning and the end of the realization.

Pure existence.

Existence doesn't need to be pure: it is absolutely independent of all notions of purity or impurity. Consciousness already depends on That what is consciousness, but That what is consciousness never needs to be aware.

There is not time.

"No time" is still too much. For That, "nothing" is too much and "everything" is not enough: it is never too much or too little. When there is nothing you are nothing, and when there is everything you are everything. And when there is neither of them you are what is without either of them.

It is the devotee's devotion and it is called Grace, Grace which doesn't know Grace by being Grace: that makes everything that is not Grace drop. It *is* Life! Nothing ever happened: by its eternal fire, by being the Self which doesn't know any Self, the Self burns all ideas in a split second. If the eternal fire sets alight the spark you think you are, there never was a spark. And only this eternal fire can do what never needs to be done.

When you are what you are, nothing ever happened and nothing must happen. When you are Knowledge, who is there to care? That can never be lost or gained. You are That what is light, and you are Silence, permanently That. So all actions or non-actions are the absolutely undifferentiated Silence.

On the Day of Pentecost, the light lights up, the Heart is initiated. When it is set alight, it burns all that is false by its very nature. Such is the Pentecost celebration, the initiation of the Spirit: the burning Heart instantly burns all the falsity of ownership.

ॐ

25
Deceived by yourself

❧

A man said to him:
Tell my brothers
to divide my father's possessions with me.
He said to him:
O man, who has made me a divider?
He turned to his disciples and said to them:
I am not a divider, am I?

Man is made for communication, whether it is with the eyes of the heart, with words or with the hands. How to find a right balance in this practice?

It needs somebody to speak of right or wrong balance.

But sharing must happen.

What must be shared?

The communication. Let's call it whatever we like.

No, it is freedom itself! With the idea that you can find That and share it, you make of it a piece of cake. Be happy that you cannot share That, because nobody owns That. You can talk and talk and talk, and nothing comes out of it. It is entertainment, the joy of talking for the sheer joy of talking. God, or Existence, doesn't need to talk. Talking is pure joy, free from all reason. Talking is pure meditation, action without expectation. The nature of consciousness is to meditate in action as in non-action without expecting to know itself: void from action and non-action, void from understanding or non-understanding. Such is the beauty of emptiness: the absence of any necessity, intention or goal. And nothing is happening.

Yet Jesus says in this logion, "I am not a divider, am I?". It still implies a true sharing. So why do we speak? Why do we have a mouth?

It is simply energy in action, but nothing happens. That doesn't need to be justified, it is always right. Existence is always right. Even when it is false, it is right. There are no mistakes for Existence. Only "I" can make mistakes. To be an "I" is already a mistake. And from the first mistake follow on all other mistakes.

The "I" imagines that he shouldn't make mistakes.

The "I" cannot imagine anything. How can an imagination imagine anything?

But you say that it is the "I" who makes mistakes.

When "what you are" takes itself for somebody, still it is Existence playing ignorant. But by playing in this way, it is not necessarily stupid. There is a phantom who plays whatever: the phantom is himself played. So it is always Existence, Knowledge, which plays ignorant, and nothing changes.

Is falling in love heading down the wrong path?

To fall in love you need two: the lover falls in love with himself, which is already false. Then you become a fallen angel, and from there you become the devil: the narcissist lover being in love with his own image.

We rightly say, "falling in love"!

Yes, you fall in love and you cannot do otherwise because trying to avoid is also a form of love. Love constantly tries to get an advantage. To love yourself is to care about what you are. No way out, impossible! And this love affair is the way you realize yourself, *ad infinitum*. You must be what you are with or without it. This is the Divine Comedy. Are you really serious when you say that you believe in yourself? What a joke! To understand the joke is to *be* the joke, and not to laugh about it is the biggest joke. Not to laugh about the joke you are makes you a serious seeker.

But the seeker is passionate, full of ardour to reach the goal, he wants to surpass himself, to merge in love!

Wanting, wanting, wanting... I want to possess my beloved, to be one with him, to entirely possess him. Unity is the biggest trap. Where there is unity, there is duality, both come together.

And if we merge?

Who? Who?

The seeker who is merging in love.

But who needs that? A phantom in unity with a phantom? Oh, no! "I am That" means being That what is Reality, and this you *are*. There is no second.

Nobody can deceive you as well as you yourself and you are constantly deceived. It makes you an absolute fool: deceived by yourself. There is no second, no Father, no God, no one who could deceive you, and you know this very well. Nobody can betray you as well as you yourself.

Is realization to understand this?

No, it is to *be* That! Understanding is still deceiving yourself. Thus the deep deep sleep is a perfect indication. Your existence doesn't need to have experiences.

All teachers say, "stay in the presence".

Yes, indeed, it is still Mephisto speaking. The devil wants to keep you in his teacher's business. Ramana Maharshi always said that the one who is called the true guru, the *satguru*, kills you instantly. But the guru who wants to enlighten you, this teacher of enlightenment who says, "you must understand, you must wake up", makes you dependent.

So wanting to wake up is already false!

It is already one too many.

And the guru who says, "I had this experience, I am showing it to transmit it to you", is he a false guru?

It is already too late. Somebody had an experience and is claiming it: "I had this realization and can share it with you. Follow me and I promise you that…". All we can say is that Existence never had any experience and whatever has an experience comes too late. Existence has no owner. Being the knower is still one experience too many. A *jnani* who knows he is a *jnani* is a *jnani* too many. A master who takes himself for a master has still to meet his master.

It is always the Self facing itself: the Self doesn't need to know why. The idea of *satguru* means that only *you* can satisfy yourself, because you are satisfaction itself and nobody can give it to you. That cannot be taught, That cannot be described, That cannot be transmitted. That doesn't need a presence, That is a total absence of necessity. It is *moksha*, freedom without anybody who is free. It is to be free of a second in a split second: by being That what is without a second, the idea of a second explodes.

❧

26
Jesus is the Living Word

❦

His disciples said to him:
Twenty-four prophets spoke in Israel,
and all of them spoke in you.
He said to them:
You have omitted the one living in your presence
and have spoken (only) of the dead.

*A*re there such things as true words?

As soon as they are repeated, they are already false. Even if we repeat them word for word, it is already false.

Then we can say that everything that Ramana Maharshi said, he has not said.

Ramana never said anything.

Everything that Jesus said is also false?

If we repeat what Jesus said, it is false, because Jesus is the Living Word. Otherwise they are like words repeated by a parrot, and they are always false. It is a parody. Jesus always indicated the Living Word, meaning: when Life speaks it is always alive. But when some one so-called alive speaks, it is always dead, his words are only a repetition: Life never repeats itself.

It is the end of booksellers and publishers.

It is the cemetery of words, the cemetery of lies: dead and empty words. As soon as they are printed they are lies. In German we say, *"er lügt wie gedruckt"*, literally, "he lies as if it was printed". My grand-father used to say: "He who writes will remain". A phantom writes his diary in the hope of remaining. The bookstores are full of biographies of the Enlightened. And 90 % of the books of the so-called Enlightened start in this way: "Once upon a time there was a non-enlightened...". It is fairy tale time: "How I woke up". Jesus didn't enter the Kingdom of the dead, he disappeared from the Kingdom of the dead and went into the Totality of Life.

You are rejecting all books and the only thing you are interested in is the Living Word. But where do you get what you say? You are not reading any more, how do you manage to have answers?

The Totality, what we call Cosmic consciousness, expresses itself in each and every word. The totality of all aspects. Who else?

I am asking this question because we can think the same of ourselves. We can all express the Totality.

I am not thinking it, I am it! You cannot *think* this. If I knew where it came from, I would be different from That, from where it came from. You are That what *is* the source. I am That what is the source. I am That what is the Absolute, and I have no problem with it. I always talk to That, from "I" to "I".

It doesn't mean that there is somebody here who is the source and talks to somebody else. It is not for no reason that it is called "the eye of God". The eye without a body, pure perception. So perception speaks to perception. But perception without the perceiver because the perceiver is already perceived. There is only perception.

I think that it is precisely because the Self talks to the Self, whether it is through Karl's form or through another form, that there is no disciple, no devotee, no worshiper. In logion 13 Jesus himself says: "I am not your master". And in logion 108:

> *He who will drink from my mouth*
> *will become like me.*
> *I myself shall become he,*
> *and the things that are hidden*
> *will be revealed to him.*

It is what is called "good company". Good company without companions, without disciples. There are only masters: it is the master in his own company.

So in that sense, you never said anything, like Buddha who spoke for forty years and never said anything.

You can say that Buddha or Jesus spoke a lot but their words were empty because no word leads to That what is Buddha. They are simply void of meaning.

But if in a hundred or one thousand years somebody repeats exactly the words you pronounce today, they will also be totally empty.

No, no, they will be full: full of intentions, the intention of the repetition, the intention of clarity. Every human word is an intention. Buddha's words belong to meditation. Every word of his is an action without intention. But every meditator who speaks to mean something, who meditates with the intention of meditating, who wants to reach the meditator through the meditation, is actually full of intentions. "This" is meditation of the Being, it is an empty action without intention, it is an *absence* of intention.

The disciple's intention is to understand but Buddha or Jesus speak behind the one who understands. They are taking you behind the light by speaking to That what is the source of the light, to That what is the Knowledge which doesn't need to understand anything to be what it is. They always speak beyond and through the one who understands.

"Whoever has ears to hear, let him hear!". How many times Jesus repeats it! I can quote logia 8, 21, 24, 63, 65, 96...

We simply talk to ourselves. And there, there is no understanding. That speaks by Itself to Itself, That understands by Itself and there is nobody who has to understand anything. It is Joy speaking and Joy listening, Joy which says nothing by speaking and hears nothing by listening. There is no one speaking and no one saying anything meaningful to another person listening, no one understanding with the idea of having an advantage. It is the absolute absence of a spirit having the slightest utility. There is absolutely no future, it is an eternal Now without any intention of future.

❧

27

Mary's realization

৯৫

LOGION 55

Jesus said:
Whoever does not hate his father and his mother
cannot become a disciple to me.
And whoever does not hate his brothers and sisters
and take up his cross in my way
will not be worthy of me.

The cross is a symbol of the impasse. The horizontal represents time and the vertical represents the Spirit. At the centre, at the intersection, it is awareness. To be nailed on the cross is to be That. There is no escape, it is peace. The cross is a symbol of peace. What is happening here and now is the crucifixion of the idea that you can escape from what you are. The crucifixion is taking place here and now, halleluiah! I find the cross to be the most relevant symbol.

When religion imprisons or limits it becomes ecclesiastical and needs a home. Then God becomes dogmatic, he becomes a watchdog who constantly has to be aware of himself to remain in absolute consciousness. Vipassana. Absolute vigilance about everything that moves. We are sitting while running in our heads. Even Buddhism is dogmatic. If Buddha were alive today he would destroy all monasteries. He would make "tabula rasa".

A guru is one who brings light, who enlightens, but he is also Lucifer, one who wants to enlighten you, who wants to help you. Lucifer is the great Saviour, he comes to your rescue: "Follow me, I will bring you the light, I promise you a house where you will feel at home". He hands you the light: it is the carrot, the carrot of enlightenment. But the devil comes out of yourself because between you and the devil there is no difference. Thus we are our own devil, our own temptation, and we cannot blame any one but ourselves. It is sheer narcissism.

After having run after the carrot we get beaten with a stick.

Yes, because we are a donkey, always led by other donkeys, which kick you with their hooves. Who is the biggest donkey?

And the Immaculate Conception?

Yes, let's talk about Mary, it is also very interesting. What is the meaning of Virgin Mary's virginity? For me, this logion speaks of Mary's realization: when Mary saw her son dying on the cross, she realized through his crucifixion that she never had a son and never had been a mother's daughter. At that moment she discovered her own virginity. It is not that the Holy Spirit came into her and she conceived Jesus. No, this is a fairy tale from the church. In fact, it is Mary's realization, the realization of the Unborn. When her mother's heart broke, Mary became the Black Madonna, the black light, the Unborn.

But the texts of the Gospels are there to testify, and they have been interpreted...

...always differently.

But in the Gospels it is written that the archangel Gabriel went to see a young woman who had not known any man, nothing is mentioned about the loss of the virginity, simply that the Spirit came into her when she was a virgin.

For me, the symbol of the Immaculate Conception is Mary's realization, the surrender of the relative love. Mary frees herself from her maternity. It is the most accomplished love because motherly love is an illusory love and for the Heart to be, it must be broken. It is unthinkable for a mother to lose the love she has for her son without her heart being broken. To my sense, Mary is a symbol of the state of a mother whose heart is broken when she loses the son she never had.

This myth of virginity was going around the Mediterranean basin: various Greek heroes had for their father a god. Hence, the virginity was self-evident.

Yes, we can explain all of this as being part of History, nevertheless I find it beautiful, when Grace allows it, that every mother loses her maternity and every father loses his identity as a father. I always find this to be a good sign of Grace, and never mind the stories going around.

Karl, what you just said refers us directly back to logion 79:

> *A woman from the crowd said to him:*
> *Blessed are the womb which bore you*
> *and the breasts which nourished you.*
> *He said to her:*
> *Blessed are those who have heard the word of the father*
> *and have truly kept it.*
> *For there will be days when you will say:*
> *Blessed are the womb which has not conceived*
> *and the breasts which have not given milk.*

✤

28
I always talk to the Absolute

❧

LOGION 51

His disciples said to him:
When will the repose of the dead come about,
and when will the new world come?
He said to them:
What you look forward to has already come,
but you do not recognize it.

The disciples' question is in time, and you say: everything you are seeking is here, not in the search.

The seeker, the search and the sought are not different in nature. That is already present. But the search will not stop, and has no reason to stop, for any one. So the realization as manifested consciousness is the inquiry of Nature, it is Nature questioning Nature, meditating on Nature. And the inquiry will go on, it is an endless meditation.

Is realization the disappearance of the knower?

No, nothing disappears. Why should anything happen? Who needs something to happen? Who needs to know?

Precisely the one who disappears...

No, he never disappears. He never appeared, how can he disappear? Only Knowledge is. There is no appearance or disappearance in Knowledge. The knower imagines that he appears. This imagination can never disappear, and anyway, who cares? "Appearance" or "disappearance" are beautiful words which convey an idea of movement, of coming and going, and this is already the dream. Never does anything appear or disappear, no birth, no death. The knower is not even born, how can he die?

Hui-Neng told us: "From the beginning not a thing is".

Nothing ever happened. If anything were to exist, there would be something in something else. So it is neither "is" nor "is not", both are ideas.

Yes, but we cannot function without ideas.

Yes, we can function, even without ideas.

But I mean in the world of human beings.

You are human only because of this idea of birth. Without this idea, where is the man? There is only the Self, Life. This is Reality.

But when I appear as a person, something is happening! Hasn't Jesus said in logion 28:

> I took my place in the midst of the world,
> and I appeared to them in flesh.

It is an experience of flesh, which can only take place because the information is already there. It is like centering a camera shot, everything is already there. Perceiving yourself as flesh is not an appearance but an experience that you are having. It is "what is already there", like a film which never was shot, an absolute block of film. So you perceive yourself in infinite possibilities but they don't appear, they are already there. They don't appear and then disappear: everything that is, is totally present.

When I, Jesus, have this experience, I am free to have it or not to have it.

No, not free.

Jesus is not free? The Absolute is not free?

No, the Absolute is freedom, but the Absolute is not free from anything. There is no second, so the Absolute cannot be free from anything. Only in the world of ideas, there can be somebody who is free from something else, therefore That can never be free. You cannot free yourself from anything, you *are* That! You are the freedom which is the Living. There is simply no second edition of Life, so you cannot be free from what you are. You *are* That, no way out!

Freedom doesn't know freedom, and freedom doesn't need freedom, because freedom is what it is. It is the beauty of the Absolute, which cannot "not be" what it is, therefore no freedom. You have to realize yourself in every experience which comes, it is unavoidable, because it is already there. The next inhalation, the next exhalation, the next sip of coffee, are unavoidable. You cannot avoid yourself and you will always realize yourself in ignorance.

Is Karl talking to the little" me" or to the Absolute?

I always talk to the Absolute. I don't talk to a phantom who can only know himself in the pain of separation. The experience will always be experienced by an experiencer different from what he experiences, there is no way out. The realization will always be an experience of separation, and what you are can never be experienced. It is the way you realize yourself: sometimes in unity and sometimes in duality, but both are separation, and it is endless, no beginning, no end.

We should remove the word "God", otherwise it is somebody's God.

God doesn't need to remove any God. The fact that nothing needs to be removed is the absolute removal of the idea that something has to be removed. It is the absolute dropping of the dropper. Nobody cares if there is somebody dropping or not dropping. Existence never cares if there is somebody worrying or not worrying. Nobody cares about what can be dropped. And if nobody cares if the devil drops the idea of God or not, what is there to drop?

The person.

Why? For whom?

Because it perpetually keeps the duality. It maintains the phantom.

So what? It is entertaining! What kind of relative existence would this be, if something had to be dropped for Existence to be?

But I don't exist.

Who says that you don't exist? Me, me, me! "Me" says, "I don't exist".

"Me" mostly says, "I don't want to suffer".

Of course, it is the nature of "me" not to want to suffer, and when he doesn't want to suffer, he suffers. So what? Let him play this game, Existence doesn't care. Only "me" is interested in the end of suffering, and because of this hope, he suffers, but nobody cares. It is a survival system: the "me" survives because he hopes that the suffering will end, what to do?

It came when it came, and it will go when it will go. But That what is the underlying Reality never cares about its presence or its absence. Only the other "me's" care about it, a community of "me's"! Me, me, me...! "Me" will always care about himself.

So all those people who speak of "letting go" are wasting their time.

Yes, like each and every one, I waste the time I don't have. What else can we waste? In any case, time is being wasted, no problem, but if we believe that we do indeed need help in easing suffering, we might as well go and see a doctor.

Existence cannot help you and has no interest in this whatsoever. The idea of helping has meaning only for a person involved in this tragicomedy, but not for That what *is* the tragicomedy. For the divine, it is simply a comedy, and the "me" is part of it, but there is no bridge: "me" will always be a drama and the divine will always be a comedy.

29
You are the infinite wonderer

Logion 90

Jesus said:
Come unto me,
for my yoke is easy
and my lordship is mild,
and you will find repose for yourselves.

It seems to me that awakening is the fruit of some work, of a long hardship, it is a slow death.

As Tibetans say, we must wear out the soles of the ego.

God awakens after he has been hypnotized by himself. It is a long story: first he is hypnotized, then he wakes up from his hypnosis, then he is hypnotized again, an endless story. Ramana Maharshi used the analogy of the spider spinning its web and trying to catch itself, then waking up from the idea of ever being able to succeed, and removing its whole web. But as soon as it is removed, it again wakes up as a spider, again starts spinning its web and trying to catch itself, and there is no end to it.

So what is the use of wanting to wake up, since as soon as we wake up, it is to be hypnotized again?

To be awake is still to be hypnotized. This is the whole question of identified and non-identified consciousness: even non-identified consciousness is part of the dream. Awakening happens only in the dream and everything that is in the dream is still asleep. Let's call it waking up from the idea of awakening: awakening will not happen. Awakening is rather: you are what you are, neither awake nor non-awake, and always in spite of everything. It is not something new, That is uninterrupted. It is not that something vanishes and after you are what you are, no! It is neither old nor new.

This is true joy, if I may say so, because we have understood that we are always what we are, no matter what happens. It is a joy and we don't seek any more.

No, you *are*, whether you seek or not. There is the Joy of not needing to be joyful, the Joy of not knowing joy. As soon as you know it, you create suffering, both come together. Happiness and unhappiness are inseparable. What you are never needs to be happy. One of the main points is: what needs to be happy will always be unhappy. What you are never needs anything. What you are never needs to wake up.

It is when we understand this that there is joy, when we realize this...

No, no, no, not when you understand this, Joy has always been there. It is not dependent on an understanding, it is in spite of all understandings, never because of... You cannot make it personal: "Can I stay a little bit personal? Can I stay a little bit awake?" No!

When two people hate each other for the rest of their lives, is it joy?

Yes! Hate and love come together, both are love. You hate only when you love.

Like Saint Paul who hated Jesus so much that he fell in love with him.

Yes, you can only hate what you love. You hate that you love yourself and you love that you hate yourself. This is daily life: you hate getting up and you love going to bed, but to love going to bed, you must hate getting up.

When the mind stops there is like a peace.

It is an *experience* of peace. There is either the experience of a person having an experience or the experience of the absence of a person. In the first case there is what is called the mind, the experiencer is different from what he experiences, and it is duality. Then there is the absence of the experiencer and of the experience, and it is unity. So no-mind is unity and mind is duality, and Existence experiences itself both ways.

If the mind stops for a split-second, am I free of it?

Yes, you are free from the separation between the experiencer and what is experienced. Then there is only the experience, you are One. In the presence of unity, you experience an ocean without waves, it is the Spirit, no-mind, the impersonal vertical experience that you call "now", no before or after. It is an advantage, because "now" seems free of suffering. In the horizontal, there is the story of before and after, the mind compares and shows itself in pairs of opposites: love and hate. This is called suffering, passion. In the vertical, there is no suffering. So there is somebody, the phantom, who feels better in the no-mind than in the mind where he feels impure. So there is pure Spirit and impure mind.

When there is neither before nor after, there is only "I", so no story, no time. It feels like Paradise: the absence of the sufferer and the absence of suffering, of psychological terror. It is not so bad but as you said, you will always fall back into the story. Every day, you continuously go from "story" to "no-story": sometimes you are personal, then perception goes to the impersonal, and sometimes even to awareness. Then everything disappears. There is either time or no-time. It constantly changes and you cannot stay here or there simply because you wish to do so.

The moment you want to stay in the verticality of Now, you are outside, it is a rule. There is nobody, but as soon as there is somebody, he is outside, and the story begins. Sometimes it happens while meditating, maybe you are sitting in Zazen, looking at the wall, and the shift happens: you wake up, you go from the personal to the impersonal. Maybe you are really lucky and you go towards That what is the screen where forms and no-forms are empty, meaning that neither unity nor duality are That. Then you are already a *jnani* who sees that form and no-form are both empty.

But neither the horizontal nor the vertical can give you the peace you are persistently seeking. There is no peace, neither in time nor in no-time. You are already awareness, yet, even from there, you may leave again: no place to land. If it were a refuge, there would still be an "I" who should land somewhere. Wherever you land, you must leave again, it is inevitably so.

When the story is there, it means that before there was a moment when you didn't understand, and now there is one when you understand. It is simply a story, and only a phantom has a story. And when the phantom understands and wakes up, then it is an awakened phantom.

All of this is a movie, pure imagination. Reality never moves, and the one who wants to stop the screening of the film is part of it: it is like wanting to stop time. And this is also a good movie: once upon a time there was an empty screen, it's a fairy tale! What to do? Just enjoy it, because the tale is endless.

A moment ago, as I was peeling potatoes, my mind calmed down and I was happy. But we cannot spend our life peeling potatoes!

Nothing is easier than That. Being what you are doesn't require anything, and being what you are is simply like peeling a potato, an infinite potato...

But if you are peeling potatoes and want to enjoy the fruits of your labour, it is too much! If you are simply peeling them, it is meditation: there is no expectation, no intention to make French fries afterwards...

Then it is attention without intention.

No, it is simply to be what is never hungry, but still you have to peel potatoes. Even if nothing can satisfy you, you must try! Do I have to repeat that love will never stop? Sometimes love is with a lover, sometimes it is without a lover, that's all, but neither can make or unmake what you are. Thus you are what you are even when there is intention. If you wait for the intention to go, you can wait for a long time...

Why this desire to constantly meditate?

Because it is your nature, your natural state. As soon as you wake up, you meditate on what you are in all possible and impossible ways, it is the way you realize yourself. It is Life living itself. So Life experiencing life is Life meditating on life. For That, there is no other way, and you cannot avoid it, because you are this Life which cannot avoid itself or avoid a single life experience. No way out! You experience yourself in pleasure and in suffering, because you cannot have one without the other. There is always an absolute balance between love and hate, light and darkness, beauty and ugliness, holiness and bestiality, wisdom and folly, a perfect balance.

Life passes through a body to experience itself in a unique way.

Every snowflake is different. Nothing or nobody is the same, always unique. Everything is the Self and everything is always different, but never different in nature. Every moment is different but the nature of the moment is always...

... like water in a snowflake?

Yes, it is an ancient Indian analogy: vapour, snowflake, ice or liquid differ in appearance but not in nature, it is what is called energy, consciousness. Energy can never be an object of experience, only its effects. The experience of energy is not energy, it is not different from energy but it is not energy. We can call it Life, always different, but never different in nature. And this is your nature, which shows itself different from the rest but never different from itself. How many times do I have to repeat it?

It's very clear!

Remove all clarity, and you remain. Remove the silence, and Silence is. Silence never discriminates between silent or not-silent, but the brain is always looking for something new, like an insatiable stomach. If you realize that awareness is your nature, then you look for something deeper, and this, *ad infinitum*. You are always behind yourself, behind the idea of Self, always hidden. Your nature will always be hidden, never exposed. You will never find yourself in the light, but always behind it. So be a mystery to yourself, and marvel! Be full of wonder, it's wonderful! And the "me", which is a mirage, is a real miracle!

❦

30
There is only Life

❧

LOGION 19

Jesus said:
Blessed is he who came into being
before he came into being.
If you become my disciples
and listen to my words,
these stones will minister to you.
For there are five trees for you in Paradise
which remain undisturbed summer and winter
and whose leaves do not fall.
Whoever becomes acquainted with them
will not experience death.

Nothing happens. By the experience of birth, nobody is born, so nobody dies.

That I am born is a story, but I never had the opportunity to see it.

You have inevitably been the witness of it, you were already there. If you don't remember, it doesn't mean that you didn't witness it. That you don't have memory doesn't mean anything. Even death can happen and you have to witness it, and nothing happens. The memory of your last death is not there either, because memory belongs to the body, like a hard disk which starts being written on at the age of three.

It is already the personal story.

Yes, because at around three years old, there is already somebody writing the story, the collector begins.

So you say that I have been the witness of something, which actually never happened.

It happened as an experience, but by this experience nothing happened. Yet you cannot say that nothing happened. Birth took place, but your nature was already there before birth and it will be there after, like it is "now", unborn in birth and not dying in death. There is this famous Zen koan: "What was your face before you were born? Did you have a face before you were born?" Even without a face, you are.

Everyone wants to have a direct personal experience of That. Thomas the Unbeliever wanted to touch Jesus' open wound with his fingers, he needed a proof, but there will never be any. If you wait for a proof, you can wait for a long time! However, doubts will never end: in each presence there is a doubt, again and again. Only when you are in deep deep sleep, in the absence, there is no doubt and no doubter. Yet, you exist!

Even to say "I don't know", you must exist. The absence of doubt must first be there for the unbeliever to doubt or not doubt, so this omnipresence is always there. It is like an "omni-*pre*-sense". Then comes the presence of the doubter who doubts or not, of the knower who knows or not. In the "*pre*-sense" of your nature, Knowledge has to be there, and it is free of doubts. Even if what you call the doubting "me" doesn't doubt in this moment, he will doubt again, starting with not-doubting! It is his survival system. The doubter can remain in separation only if he doubts himself. He can only survive in the story of doubt and no-doubt.

What do you mean by doubting oneself?

The experience of being always remains doubtful. The moment somebody exists, he constantly doubts his own existence, because sometimes he is there and sometimes not. So he is there, and he is not there. He appears, and he disappears, it is the nature of the phantom. If he were real he would be there uninterruptedly. Only Existence has no interruption.

He is not there when he is in deep sleep.

In deep sleep there is nobody, but who is this guy who appears in the morning, and where was he? He is there only when memory is there, only when there is an experience. But where is he when there is no experience? So he is there, and he is not there.

Who sleeps in deep sleep?

In this moment nobody is awake. There is nobody now as there is nobody in deep sleep, there is only Life. In this moment there is a dream body, a dream "I", and in deep sleep there is no dreamer. But Existence is always present, so Nature is there but the experience of "I", where is it? It is what is called the phantom. You can say, That what is your nature is always there, but in the absence of "I" Nature has no "I". So the presence of "I" is sometimes there and sometimes not. It is the nature of the phantom to doubt his nature, because his presence will always remain doubtful.

There is no consciousness in this body, it is consciousness, it is energy, and there is nobody. Whether this space is consciousness or this body is consciousness, where is the difference? Consciousness is matter, consciousness is no-form and consciousness is awareness, where is the difference? They are different aspects of consciousness, different experiences. It is what I call the realization of Reality, which is not different from Reality.

People are always fascinated by what was there before birth and what will come after. The reason for this is fear: "What will happen?". Since there is an idea, an imagination that something uncontrollable could happen, you want to know what is going to happen. You want to control every moment, out of fear of being yourself controlled. It is the phobia of the doubting phantom, what else can he do?

A master tells us how to stop that.

How to "be quiet", not how to stop, to stop is already too much action! Be what you are, this is what the master tells you. Be what you cannot not be, be That, the nature of which is Silence. So be quiet and see, because you cannot not see. Perception has to perceive, and perception perceives first the perceiver, knower or non-knower, and then what can be perceived. But perception is always Silence, never disturbed or stained by what is happening, immaculate. So perception is closer to your nature, but you will never know *what* it is.

In deep sleep, there is nobody that perceives.

The absence of the perceiver doesn't mean that there is no perception. For the perceiver to be perceived when he wakes up in the morning, perception must be there.

You cannot find the perceiver. The perceiver you find is already perceived. The experiencer is already experienced. You can only say: for somebody to be alive, Life must be there. For the experience of an experiencer to be, energy or Life, which manifests itself in the experiencer, must already be there. Without this energy, without this Living, no experiencer could be there.

For a Creator to be, or whatever, That what is life must be prior. For the Living to be able to manifest itself as the Creator, as the Father, It must be prior to its manifestation. Then comes the Spirit, then "the man and the world". Thus you can say that the nature of God is Life, but not the experience of God. So Life first realizes itself as the realizer, then as the Spirit, then as the manifestation of the whole universe.

Whether the body is there or dead, it is always the experience of Life. Is there a difference?

There are always differences, but Life doesn't become more or less. Life never knows itself as such. Whatever it knows, it is never it: it is neither the presence nor the absence, neither this nor that, and this is the true practice of neti-neti. Same for the Tao: whatever you say about it, it is never it: it is neither the presence nor the absence, neither this nor that. It is Buddha's middle way: yes and no. You can't even say, "it is not that", because it is "yes and no", always undecided, without any specific shape. It expresses itself in infinite ways, but doesn't have any way Itself.

A book came out some time ago, called "Zen, the biggest Lie of all times". If you call That, "Life", it is a lie, if you call That, "Nature", again it is a lie, any name is wrong! But finally, who cares? You are lying anyway, whatever can be said is a lie, so who cares? You might as well give it a name.

What makes life is the need to have experiences, but if all experiences have already been done, if everything has been fulfilled?

There will still be the next moment. This moment has already been lived infinite times. The next moment, already lived, will be a déjà vu, which will repeat itself *ad infinitum*. Yet it is always fresh, always new, because there is nobody to memorize. Life has no memory and every moment is totally fresh although it has been lived infinite times, eternally young, never appearing or disappearing. That never gets old, it is as fresh as the morning dew, moment to moment.

At night you don't create stories, but when you wake up, you wonder what happened in your absence. You want to make it "your" absence, you claim that something happened, and it will not stop. The claimer will be erased, but not by himself. Every night he is dropped and Life is simply there. And in the morning he pops up again and may try to understand what happened during deep sleep:

"When I am not there, it must be my true nature". It is natural, it is looking for the biggest love.

I am always sorry to have to destroy everything, but what else can I do? Whatever you say, I will take the opposite point of view and destroy both. Here, nothing can remain.

❧

31
There will never be
a happy dream

❧

LOGION 66

Jesus said:
Show me the stone
which the builders have rejected.
That one is the cornerstone.

The root thought "I", which holds the whole story, is this central point linking all that is around. If you remove it by being what is prior to it, the whole house is burning, because in the fire of the Heart, the Living fire, no house can stay. All false houses are burnt down in That what is the house. It is as if you would lose the anchor holding your ship: where would you be? You would simply explode in what you are.

The root thought "I", is it the carpet that you are constantly pulling from under our feet?

Yes, it is the carpet, your favourite place!

Everything is a concept.

But you are holding on to the concept that all is a concept, you are only changing concepts. 'No concepts' is still a bloody concept!

No way out! Actually, "me" is a thought that we cannot see: when we look for it, we don't find anything.

Under the carpet, there are only wind and dust, but you will hide there. "Me" is most cunning, most intelligent, it is the logos itself, it will always find a place to hide. Sometimes he says, "I am Nothingness", and sometimes, "I am All", or, "My nature is unity". He always hides behind beautiful words. He might even hide in darkness, where you cannot see him. He is so tricky, this "me", that you cannot catch him. The moment you want to grab him, he has disappeared. So, where is he?

If we focus on what we are really feeling, for example emotions, we don't find anything. In fact, only inattention creates suffering. If we really focus attention on something, there is no beginning or end.

It is part of the game. Anyway, whether you focus attention or not, it disappears. Your attention may have some control: it is consciousness, which is always seeking pleasure, and pleasure is the absence of pain. It is always a good intention. Loving, caring about our pleasure, our happiness, is natural, and it is the absence of suffering, but there will always be a new suffering somewhere. There are only temporary solutions, so there is no happiness, there is not even happiness in happiness.

Because at that time you are not in the present moment?

In the present moment there is nobody.

I enjoy, but I know that something is going to fall on my head.

You already know that it is not going to last. But when you are miserable you think that it is going to last for ever, fantastic! You distrust happiness and only trust unhappiness. Actually you are right: even Buddha, when he was asked if suffering will end, was saying no. Every experience is suffering, you can only experience suffering. Happiness, your nature, can never be felt.

So joy, the happiness you are, will never be an experience, and the happiness that you can experience is part of suffering. Therefore you must be what you are in spite of suffering. There will never be an end to ignorance or knowledge, and since you cannot find knowledge in ignorance or happiness in suffering, who cares? But this underlying peace is uninterrupted. So the worst case-scenario, that you will never be happy, is not so bad, because it pulls the carpet from under your feet, the idea that you can do something to find happiness, and this "doing" is hell. But you cannot *not* seek happiness: as I said, your natural intention is happiness. Your natural intention is to discover Reality.

Outside.

Yes, but it doesn't matter, even inside is false. It is false outside and it is false inside. To imagine that it can be found is hell!

Buddha said, "I see the search for nirvana as a nightmare in daytime".

Yes, it is a permanent nightmare. There will never be a happy dream.

Precisely, it may not be necessary to let go.

There never was the slightest need. Nobody needs to cut his head off to be what he is. Actually, *this* is chopping off the head: cutting the idea that something needs to be cut off. It is the absolute cut, the split second: to be in spite of this cut or in spite of all that can be cut off. Then, whether the phantom exists or not, who cares? This is *truly* killing the phantom, because it is precisely because somebody tries to kill him that he exists!

You imagine that you can be happy only in the presence of the phantom, but if you are what you are anyway, nobody cares if the phantom is there or not, not even you! This radically cuts the idea that something has to disappear, and this can be done only by the Self, by being the Self, and by knowing no Self. By being what you are, all that is known… "Bye, Bye!". Even if it is there, it is a total "Goodbye!".

If somebody tells me, "You should give up this aspect of your personality", it hurts.

Yes, he is a butcher. If he tries to cut off something from you, it hurts. He wants to dominate you, to make of you the doll he wishes you to be. Existence never asks anything from you. This is discrimination: the one who asks you to be different, to know more, to go deeper, to open your heart, etc., is not That. Life takes you as you are. There is no right or wrong moment. You are as absolute as you must be. This total acceptance from Totality is Peace. Nobody can give it to you and no special behaviour, good or bad, can take you there. So God, in his nature, never asked you to be different. You don't have to keep quiet or not to keep quiet. God never demanded anything from you, only the devil who needs your soul, your attention: "I can help you, but please, look at me".

Can I sell my soul only to the devil, not to God?

You can only sell the soul you don't have to the devil who doesn't exist, not bad, isn't it? What a fabulous game! Nothing to gain, nothing to lose, just for fun, it is great entertainment!

You are the origin of God and of the devil. As soon as you know yourself, there is a knower and a non-knower, and one who wants to teach you. Thus it is *you* who creates all of this, and the moment there is a creator, he creates: Christ and anti-Christ, and there is a crisis, but it is the way you realize yourself, in polarities. No way out! Therefore there is a devil, there is a God, and there is neither one nor the other!

So duality is a necessity.

Absolutely. Good needs evil, night needs day. Love and hate are inseparable, no way out!

But only in the manifestation.

Yes, but it is what you are, you are good and you are evil.

Is there duality between the Absolute and the manifestation?

No, because you *are* That. You are That what is good and That what is evil. You are That what is beauty and you are That what is ugliness. You cannot find what you are not.

Is Reality always there in the manifestation?

No, it is never there. If it were present, That would be part of something else. It is That what is presence but it is never present, so this can never be felt. This is omnipresent but not present. "Presence" is already That what you are, experiencing itself as presence.

Presence is good, but not good enough. That is why so many people stay stuck in this "Now" of awareness. Those who refer to the "power of the present moment" speak from a reference point, which would be preferable to another point, so different. Then it is hell. Any reference point is a point too many, it cannot be That. So Peace is not reachable in the presence either. It is not bad but it is not good enough for what you are. Even this presence cannot fulfil you absolutely. Simply be That what doesn't need to be fulfilled, and it is satisfaction itself.

You cannot rest anywhere. You can only rest in That what never needs to rest. So in this resting place of "Now", no rest, it is like a big buffet which will never be hearty enough to satisfy you, *"La Grande Bouffe"*!

I am this "me" looking for the absence of "me", and this makes me suffer.

Yes, "me" wants to get rid of "me".

Yet there are moments when we may not feel this suffering.

Yes, when you are sleeping, every night you are absent. Everybody likes this deep deep sleep.

By accepting our mental or even physical suffering, we can come to bear...

...this cannot be done. Simply by being what you are, there is acceptance, but your relative acceptance will never be enough. There will always be a camel to step on your foot and your tolerance limit will be crossed. You can train yourself to accept, but it will be a false acceptance. Existence will show you its value: none. Therefore what you call "my acceptance", the acceptance you can possess, has no value at all.

So what to do with suffering?

I don't know... take a pain killer, I am not a doctor! No, there is only one Absolute solution: the fact that there will never be any! Then the patient is not there, and never was. You cannot find the sufferer, because he is there only in the hope that suffering ends. "Me" lives on hope!

❧

32
Everything I say
is part of the dream

࿐

LOGION 43

His disciples said to him:
Who are you, that you should say these things to us?
(Jesus said to them)
You do not realize who I am
from what I say to you,
but you have become like the Jews,
for they (either) love the tree and hate its fruit
(or) love the fruit and hate the tree.

Karl, who are you? Speak to us of your awakening. You often refer to an episode of the Mahabharata, which seems to have triggered your awakening.

Awakening? Not really. It was just an understanding, it was not final.

Yet you said, I quote: "...at this moment, explosion-like through the back of my head, pure light filled my perception. This was a moment of absolute acceptance of being. Time stopped, Karl and the world had disappeared and a kind of Is-ness in a glaring light appeared, a pulsating silence, an absolute aliveness, in itself perfect - and I was that".

Yes, it was indeed the end of the migraines. It broke the resistance, but it was more a phenomenon relative to the body. The controller was shattered. The third eye, the one who wanted to know That, this wish, burnt down at once. We could call this the opening of the third eye. The understanding which occurs devours the controller, then goes down to the heart.

Nevertheless there was an event, which was not deliberately triggered. Did it happen naturally, without Karl's doing?

The movie initiated this energetic breakthrough. The energy woke up, then shattered this "me", this resistance, but I cannot say that it was an awakening, because the perception didn't wake up there. It was still an experience in the dream: the resistance broke.

Resistance to what?

The attempt to know oneself. The desire to control. From then on the body experienced harmony, but it was not the awakening to who I am: as I said, it affected the body, like a physiological breakthrough, and after that I never had migraines any more; headaches, of course, but not those daily migraines, not this stabbing pain.

If I could talk about something final, it would rather be eight or ten years later, in presence of the mountain Arunachala, with Shiva's light, because until then I was still in awareness, I had made it my home. But with Arunachala, it was more subtle: it was seeing that light is already a sensation, and being prior to light in the cave of the Heart. Not an awakening, but simply, "Ahaa...". Before, it was still like a very stunning energetic firework, but this "ahaa...", more substantial and irreversible, didn't create any physical reaction. Before, it could still be taken personally, but then, it was impossible.

I could have stayed stuck in this light, then I would have become a teacher of light, and actually, until then, I was like that. And I would say: "You must wake up and be the light, when you have this breakthrough, you feel harmony, because there is unity with everything". But for me, this "ahaa..." is more substantial, ahaa!

You are telling us that most of those who claim to be awakened remain in awareness, believing it is final. They have no notion of something prior, and they teach as if they knew the truth.

Yes, they made it their home, because it is comfortable. But I don't criticize any one: for them, it is reality.

You had been believing it for eight years, but there was still an episode.

Yes, accidentally, not intentionally, it was totally comfortable. It is not a need, but rather as if one were stumbling over it.

The last carpet... Nisargadatta also said that we must transcend awareness.

Yes, in his book, "I am That", he was referring to this "I am", to awareness, but later he said: "Forget it". I did the same: during those eight years I said, "Oh, yes, that's it!", and after, "Forget it!". You are blinded by light and don't even know it.

But you are warning us.

Warning? No. From the light there is still a possibility of returning, but from the prior, it is impossible: it is irreversible. In the light you still can take it personally, and the moment you want to stay there, you are outside. It is the last relative form where you can enter, but the prior is always prior.

At that point we see that what we would call awakening is part of the dream.

Yes, of course, it is the dream, it has to be part of the dream, *any* impression is part of the dream, anything! The *shakti*, the *siddhis*, the presence of peace, whatever you can experience in this presence is a dream: those intense energies, those vibrations, all of this is good, but...

Is Karl in a state of helplessness where he cannot even make miracles?

Yes, I am the absence of power, the absence of absence of power. Energy itself has no power, so I have no tools, and no interest either, that is the main point. Even if there were an interest, I couldn't do otherwise. This helplessness...

It is an absolute surprise to be the origin and not being able to imagine what you imagine. The next moment is the next moment, and the closest is this immense Peace, uninterrupted and unshakable, and the total absence of any demand, of any necessity of a change, it is totally natural.

Do you feel any emotions?

I feel everything! I feel the Whole, I feel all aggressions, all the things you said, people attacking me, all this energy that unfolds, but what to do? But this, I could not take it on me, it just comes and goes. You cannot bear this compassion, you cannot take it personally, it consumes you. In fact, I take it absolutely personally, in this way it doesn't make any problem. Otherwise, if you don't have an armour, you go straight to the mental hospital. Nobody has any idea of what it means.

So there are more sensations than I could imagine. Actually, it is not always easy for this body. Maybe without this breakthrough, without this energetic preparation of the cells, the body couldn't bear it. So with all the things that occurred in the 60's, these energetic teachings, these dreams in the night, this shamanism, these electric-shocks, consciousness was preparing the tool, so it's ok...

Ramana Maharshi said that if it were to come all of the sudden, like a power of 40.000 volts, it would burn you. So there is a preparation of the body.

For the body there is a preparation, that's what I am saying. When awakening happens, it is for the body, for the cells, but not for what you are. The body is prepared for what you are, but you yourself are not getting ready for anything, what to do?

"Between metanoia and paranoia", Émile used to say, "the difference is as fine as a hair!"

It is very similar, there is a very fine line! No ego is sane enough to bear it, therefore we speak of crazy wisdom. Wisdom is folly and folly is wisdom, and it is the absence of any direction of Life: no direction, no order, total chaos! To be touched by that, even a little, scares people, they feel it as an absolute abyss.

If it is supposed to happen, it will happen, and only Existence knows what is supposed to happen. What you think you are cannot get ready for this, neither you nor anyone, but That what is the Self knows best, and if Grace is after you, there is no escape. Thus it is said that if you are after Grace, you cannot find it, but if Grace is after you, Grace is everywhere!

No matter what, we cannot escape what we are.

You can neither escape nor not escape, and it is not something special, I would even say the opposite. Until this subtle "ahaa" there was always others' reactions, because I was like a walking *shakti*, which I even used. That is why I say that the controller was still there, although more subtle, maybe. There was always an advantage to be there, so it was quite special.

The last guru, which we call the *satguru*, is the guru with whom you disappear. He takes you beyond, where no teacher and no disciple can remain. And if this happens, it is because it is part of the plan, in spite of all you already did or didn't do, because what you do or don't do is already part of it, so it is unavoidable. If it is supposed to happen, it will surely happen, otherwise it will be impossible, even if you want it with all your strength. So you must be what you are even without this. Better not wait, because all this is a dream, even what I just said about this subtle "ahaa"...

For the listener...

No, even for the one who says it! Everything I say is part of the dream, even when I speak of the 4th, 5th, 6th and 7th states. None of it can bring you what you are looking for. It looks promising but it brings nothing, amazing, isn't it? So I cannot be proud of anything, no matter in which state or in which way the experiences take place. There is no rest anywhere, not even in the beyond. Neither rest nor peace, neither in the presence nor in the absence. Peace cannot be found or possessed, that is certain.

To know that there is nothing to seek, nothing to do, is nevertheless a kind of peace.

It is and will always be Peace, but not the peace you can have or the peace you can experience. I speak of all those different ways simply to show you that: whether you seek or not, you will never find. You must be what you are without an experience of peace, and you will always come to this. And if it is not your case, look at others, those seven billion experiencers, all are what you are! As personal, you may go to the 4th state, or to any other state, but what is with you in all other cases? There will never be this experience of final peace, "I realize myself and all is finished". No, it goes on, again and again! The seven states are all ignorance, because they are all different.

But in essence, there is the basis underlying them.

Yes, That underlies separation, unity, all seven states, but there is no state where you are closer. There is no way to come closer: you are not further here or closer in another state, whatever it may be. You cannot come closer to what you are, not even to the light of the beyond. Actually I am happy that nothing is final, that all is false, I like that! I am perfectly happy that what I am cannot be found anywhere. There is an absolute gratitude of not having to thank any state to be what I am. I am absolutely in spite of all, I am neither beyond nor prior, nor anything at all. I absolutely don't know what I am or what I am not, so what?

This one who is speaking, I would like to say, is the source, and with these seven states, he tells the way back from the manifestation to the source. And obviously, all the states he describes cannot be satisfying for the source itself: it is totally false, as is the whole manifestation.

There is no way back. The fact that you can return somewhere is an illusion, no way out, no way back!

Jesus says in logion 77: "From me did the all come forth / and unto me did the all extend". And in logion 49: "For you are from it, and to it you will return". I was trying to find a parallel between what Karl describes and those words from Jesus that I am trying to interpret properly. I know, it is always the mind…

I would say: you experience forgetting who you are, and you experience remembering it, but by the experience of forgetting you didn't forget it, and by the experience of remembering you don't remember it. You are always what you are in spite of the experience of forgetting and remembering yourself, so in going astray you don't go astray and in returning you don't return, so yes and no. As an experience, there is going astray and returning, but it is not real. No experience can make you or unmake you, but in this dream, you dream that you leave and that you return. It is a dream-like leaving and a dream-like returning, but in reality you never left what you are for one instant.

Actually, when I hear this, I start seeking again something that I think I lost.

Yes, seek, if it is supposed to happen this way. I can only point that out. I cannot prevent anyone from seeking. If the search must happen, it will happen. You cannot stop loving yourself and this love makes you care about your well-being, what to do? And when there is suffering you try to get out of it, but you always remain what you are. You cannot change the dream, and all of this is the way you dream and realize yourself. And it is always different: sometime relative, you experience yourself as relative to something else; and sometime you experience yourself as One with the Whole;

and then you are in the experience of the light of awareness. Then you experience yourself beyond. Next you come back as awareness, then as pure space, beyond even these indescribable seven states which the intellect cannot grasp, and everything is a dream!

We come back to this famous "What to do?". Wherever you go, you have to leave again. Whatever state you are landing in, sooner or later you will have to leave it. You can wander from one state to another, you already went through all possible states infinite times. I would call these states "the different rooms of the absolute house", where there is nobody, that's the main point. You are the house, but there is nobody home, only the *experience* of somebody who wanders through different dimensions. No wandering will make you find your nature.

Isn't it enough to understand that time is unreal to get free from all states? Because without time there can be no state or change.

But no-time is still the opposite of something else, and who understands this? Who needs it? You have to make a difference between the horizontal and the vertical where there is no time. No-time is good, it is already the "power of the present moment", but who needs this advantage? It is always the main question, who needs it? Everything that can be discriminated is not That. This is Buddha's discrimination, the noble Truth of discrimination.

On the other hand we cannot help this to happen, we constantly return, there is always going and coming back.

As I said, you cannot stop seeking, the inquiry will never end.

Even beyond this body?

Before this body, this happened infinite times. Consciousness will always look for consciousness, because it is already the dream, and in the dream, consciousness will always try. That what is consciousness never needs anything, but consciousness being conscious, or whatever, starts to dream and always realizes itself as "love, lover and beloved", it is unavoidable. Existence, which knows itself as consciousness, is already ignorant of its nature.

When this body is of no more use, it takes another one. Illusion must go on...

No problem, it is as if crash-test dummies were trying to find Absolute love. Romeo and Juliet must die instantly, because if Romeo were to live, let's say another year, he would marry somebody else. All those romantic stories are but romances with oneself. Nobody can stop this romantic sentimentalism for oneself, and nobody needs to. It is simply the way Reality shows itself, and there will be no end. No "happy end" for yourself, it has never started and it will never end. This is the happy end, the end of the idea of "end".

LOGION 91

They said to him:
Tell us who you are
so that we may believe in you.
He said to them:
You read the face of the sky and of the earth,
but you have not recognized
the one who is before you,
and you do not know how to read this moment.

❧

33
Bon voyage!

❧

He said:
O Lord, there are many around the drinking trough,
but there is nothing in the cistern.

A re we awake dreamers?

No, you are the Absolute dreamer and you dream the dreamer, but the dreamer is already part of the dream. The Absolute dreamer cannot be found in the dream, it is called Reality. And the dream is the realization of Reality, which cannot be found in any particular place. The illusion is to believe that you will find Reality in the dream.

Same thing with the seven different states, which are the dream: none of them is more real than the other. The dream is to think that Reality is different from something else, that it must be a *special* reality, that is the illusion. Wanting to make Reality special is the specialty of "me" or of the devil, because in this way he himself becomes special. And when you are special you suffer, one leads to the other. By your arrogance, you are separate, you are no more the Whole but a simple particle, and you compare your particle to another particle. This is the way you become "particular", ha ha ha!!!

We could say that the dream is the difference, and that men cultivate differences.

I think that God cultivates differences and men are already *part* of the differences, so you cannot blame them. There never were any men who did anything. You don't blame a tool, a tool never killed anyone. A machine gun never killed anyone, and the person behind the machine gun either.

Is it God who is permanently dreaming?

You can call that God, the Absolute dreamer, there are many names. "Self" is the most neutral, because this word doesn't refer to any religion. If you call that God, you start saying "My God is better than yours". The perceiver and the perceived are but a fiction, but you cannot say that perception itself is a fiction. Even for dreaming, you need to perceive. First there is the perception, then comes the perceiver.

When you say, "be what you cannot not be", is it to be aware of that?

No, it is to be with or without awareness, because you *are* with or without awareness. In any case, you can do whatever you want, it doesn't make any difference, so enjoy, have fun, because the journey is going to last quite a while! And if I say, "Bon voyage!", it is because you will never reach the final destination, this journey is endless. You may stop in the night, but in the morning you resume your journey. And death is exactly the same: the story seems to stop and you find yourself in a station, happy to have left the train, but as soon as another train comes, you are so eager to know who is inside, then hop!... you are already in the carriage! You cannot help being curious: "Who is coming?", and it is already too late. Yet it was so good to rest, to be the station itself, unmoving: "No, no, I don't move, I stay where I am", then hop!... too late!

It is what is called "the child of God": he will always be curious for the next moment. When you die all memories disappear, good and bad: you enjoy your nakedness. But as soon as your attention turns to something, it is too late: a beautiful coat goes by, and hop!... you go shopping. And as soon as you have got a beautiful coat, you want another one, then you compare: "Which one is the nicest?". You want to look good, you look at yourself in the mirror: "How do I look with this coat?". Look how consciousness plays!

Next you want to undress again, you try to do a striptease, you go to the Himalayas to forget all these stories, to become a hermit, but even in the Himalayas there are only liars... In any case, from the beginning you are a liar, and nobody cares. As soon as you say that you are aware, you are lying... Oh, time is up? So, my dear liars, thank you for coming and thank you for going!

❦

34
In the tiger's mouth!

꙳

Jesus said:
I have cast fire upon the world,
and see,
I am guarding it until it blazes.

Talking about That, hearing about That, is what Ramana Maharshi called the highest *tapas*, the highest practice. Simply hearing about That, you are in the tiger's mouth, and That will take everything away from you. All those beautiful understandings will be consumed by Grace, which shows no mercy. Grace doesn't know Grace and doesn't need any Grace. It will tear all your precious pearls, all your intellectual gymnastics, pfft! Fiction! It plays with you like with a mouse, but it is not hungry. If it kills you, it is just by accident: "Oh, sorry!"

Logion 59

Jesus said:
Take heed of the living one while you are alive,
lest you die and seek to see him
and be unable to do so.

www.ingramcontent.com/pod-product-compliance
Lightning Source LLC
Chambersburg PA
CBHW062219080426
42734CB00010B/1956